REVOLUTION BY LOVE

EMERGING ARAB YOUTH VOICES

EDITED BY DALA GHANDOUR, EMNA BEN YEDDER, MOHAMMED MASBAH, AND STEVE PARKS

REVOLUTION BY LOVE

EMERGING ARAB YOUTH VOICES

EDITED BY DALA GHANDOUR, EMNA BEN YEDDER, MOHAMMED MASBAH, AND STEVE PARKS

Ahmed Abdelhakim Hachelaf
Raghda Abushahla
Muna Abbas Ali AlBuloushi
Shatha Al-Harazi
Samah Elmeri
Dala Ghandour
Mirelle Karam Halim
Shadin Hamaideh
Mohammed Masbah
Amal Matar
Salma Nazzal
Ibrahim Yousif Shebani
Emna Ben Yedder

Revolution By Love: Emerging Arab Youth Voices

Editors:
Dala Ghandour
Mohammed Masbah
Emna Ben Yedder
Steve Parks
Lindsey Banister
Tamara Issak
Theresa Magdelena Keicher

Designer: Jesse L. Campbell

New City Community Press Mission Statement
Our mission is to provide opportunities for local communities to represent themselves by telling their stories in their own words. We document stories of local communities because we believe their voices matter in addressing issues of national and global significance. We value these stories as a way for communities to reflect upon and analyze their own experience through literacy and oral performance. We are committed to working with communities, writers, editors and translators to develop strategies that assure these stories will be heard in the larger world.

newcitycommunitypress.com

ISBN: 978-0-9840429-9-9

To Arab youth striving for dignity, freedom and justice…

CONTENTS

INTRODUCTION

"Young Souls"

This book is all about a special chemistry that sometimes manifests in a group, a deep intimacy that makes you wonder how and why a certain type of people met at a certain place and time of history.

Simply put, this story reveals how Young Arab women and men from the Middle East and North Africa, who come from very diverse backgrounds, regions, continents, share the same passion for their countries, the same audacity of hope for a better tomorrow, the same dream of making their country proud of them. All of the writers who were committed to this project were deeply convinced that one should not ask what their country will do for them, but rather what could they offer for their countries. In a world where barriers are constantly being erased, where virtual communication turns the world to a global village, what is this strange bond that ties this Arab youth to politics and public affairs?—Especially when we consider how the Western youth is moving away from this sphere.

Why would they risk their money, career, time, and life for an uncertain goal that is the so-called future of a nation? Why would they care about their fellow citizens, when they could have the choice of going abroad and have a better life? So many questions that are evoked by this project bring us to a particular shared belief: the love for a land is something sacred and inexplicable, it is who we are and whether we want it or not it, we do have some of the traits of the people of our country, we share the same collective memory, history, humor... We belong to a place that we call home, we identify with a certain kind of people, and it is part of our identity. One of the strongest aspects of this identity is that it has solid roots and it is an on-going process of improvement and added experiences. What we find so beautifully attractive about this identity of "Young Souls" is that we can always influence this identity by aspiring to new concepts that will help to shape the future. What is so imminently dangerous in this word is that if we leave it untouched, it could then become a prison.

When the people talked about their experiences, places where they lived, people they met, problems they faced and hopes they had, there was an excited spark, an irresistible light and sometimes unseen tears drops that would take the listener into the depths of their world. In their eyes, one could see the window of the future, the pride of belonging, the strength of will and the beauty of dreams. They dared to dream big, to incorporate the dream in their profession: educator, lawyer, researcher, journalist. Indeed, any profession was used as a way to participate in building a better citizen, thus a better nation. For them, any event would be another opportunity to be an ambassador for their people to the world, thus a messenger for their civilizations. All conversations led to discussions about how to improve life conditions by education, culture, infrastructure and strategy. This special energy that was moved by such a rare motivation was a remarkable engagement, a real thirst for knowledge, and an unstoppable faith in tomorrow, which made us think that there must be something special about this sort of political engagement.

It is evident that each writer who was committed to this project and thus the well-being of their nation and peoples, had an untold, unusual story that is worth sharing with the world. Maybe an anecdote, event or a particular figure, that made them do what they do now. It could even give the reader a more nuanced understanding of the people who are behind this so-called phenomenon of the 21st century: The *Arab Spring*. This mysterious, catchy, used and reused phrase, in every current political analysis of the MENA was made by the people, for the people. We invite you to discover some of the actors, and, in doing so, to demystify potent cultural myths and taboos. It is also important to mention here that not all the Arab countries experienced their spring yet, but they simply lived it differently.

What happened in the Arab World?

There is an increasing academic debate about factors and causes of Arab upheavals which started in the beginning of 2011, many answers to this phenomenon have been offered up, but most of them are based on old paradigms to understand Arab societies. The lack of understanding, the failure to recognize the specificity of the Arab revolution, is a feature of several studies about the Middle East, especially the scientific agenda that is related to the Middle East, which was already cuffed/tied by certain subjects and scoops: acutely political Islam and its radical elements, women issues, development studies... This partial knowledge, which failed to take into consideration the broad societal changes, leads to ignorance of profound changes within Arab societies; this then prevents researchers from an objective view and understanding of internal dynamics of these societies, which helps to indicate a profound crisis in the paradigm of Middle Eastern studies. The need to change or modify this approach to Middle Eastern studies should be more complex and profound; indeed, it should allow, facilitate and promote, a deeper understanding and explanation of Arab societies.

In this attempt to select some elementary factors which served as the catalysts for profound changes in the Arab Societies, we can list Three Major Factors:

1. New Media
2. Education
3. Demographic transition

There is no doubt that the New Media has had an influence on the Arab Spring movements, particularly, the new social media such as Facebook, Twitter, etc. and the international channels, such as Aljazeera. From Morocco to Bahrain, the Arab world has been witnessing the rise of an independent vibrant social media where the citizen's engagement with the Internet and its resources is steadily increasing and is expected to attract 100 million Arab Internet users by the 2015.[1] These social media resources were used by the protesters to mobilize their discourses and transmit the messages to wider audiences in the Arab world, as well as the world as a whole. Also, these social networking web-sites were the only resources for marginal groups to use, call and put forth their claims; these web-sites helped in the organization of rallies with low costs, reaching broad audiences inside and outside their own country. Citizens used these resources rather than the classical media technologies, like television or radio broadcasts, that are being monopolized by the actual governments. Until now, the Internet has been distant from the governmental control or the State monopoly – it is a "no man's land" media. But some Arab governments and decision-makers are going to start to apply pressures to make and enforce restrictions on Internet

---

[1] Jeffrey Ghannam, Social Media in the Arab World: Leading up to the Uprisings of 2011, the Center for International Media Assistance, February, 2011, p. 4

use, as he Google CEO has warned six months after the beginning of the Arab Spring that there is a potential increase of Internet censorship after the Arab Spring movements.[2]

Fatima Mernissi, renowned Arab sociologist, narrated a wise story for us about the technology expansion in the Arab society, in both rural and urban areas. She owned a statuette; it was a peasant wearing traditional clothes that was riding on his donkey and having a laptop in his hands. When she saw it for the first time, she did not understand its symbolic meaning (and neither did we in the beginning). When she asked the artisan who created it, he answered her in an ironic manner: "Really you do not know him? It is the tool of the Revolution. You have all the information in your hands; you have the world in your hands." She was surprised of this idea that was thought up by a simple artisan who was aware of the importance of technology in the actual world, and how people's lives are affected by it – as a tool of change. It implies the famous Latin idea *scientia potentia est* ("knowledge is power"). People in the Arab region are becoming more and more aware of technology's importance in their struggles for "emancipation" from the political despotism they have been living under for decades.

Education and technology are essential but not sufficient reasons for Arab revolutions; technology is not only a tool, rather it is also a culture: a culture of "emancipation" and of "knowledge sharing" among the people. This is especially true when we think about the era of "WikiLeaks Cables." This particular

---

[2] Google chairman warns of censorship after Arab Spring, BBC News US&CANADA, 27 June 2011, http://www.bbc.co.uk/news/world-us-canada-13935470

technological phenomenon released thousands of classified documents that were written by political leaders across all Arab regions, from Morocco to Saudi Arabia, passing Tunisia and Egypt. WikiLeaks' contributions are also reflected in the Arab world, and today the population of this region has become more conscious about their civil rights. The people know the two faces of their leaders, i.e. what they say in their closed cabins in contrast to what they say to their population. In sum, Arabs are increasing their knowledge not only about what they want but also what they *need*.

However, what has happened in the Arab world in the end of 2010 and in the beginning of 2011 is not a direct effect of the new media – as some journalists and columnists argued. Despite new media's importance and effectiveness, the changes were generated from the previous political and economical currents. Political and social actors have played a significant role by acting, thinking, and feeling about their current situation in the society and about their futures. In this context of social revolution, actors' claims, under the support of several social categories, some call it "population", for more freedom, dignity and social justice.

The new youth movements in the Arab world are a product of post-independence in the public schools, which has succeeded social accession of new rural generations. This development in education (knowledge capital) was not followed by an accumulation of social influence (social capital); indeed, for a long time the youth were in a disadvantaged position while attempting to access the available resources. As a result, they were marginalised in the participatory decision-making processes. This development at the educational level, which has produced new established elites, coincided with the technological development, which became available for an important segment of society that had been deprived from it for a long time. Today, most of the technological products are available in Arab Countries, at the same time as in the developed countries; the new technologies have become cheaper and more accessible for wider social categories, especially for the educated people, both from rural and urban area, who are now fortified by "formal education" and "technological development". Today we can say that the Arab youth has, so to speak, the entire world in their hands, and they escape the direct control of Institutions (State, family…). As a result, they can discover social reality on their own and in their own terms, i.e. the young generations can be informed about what is happening in other Arab countries via Aljazeera, but also via their Facebook pages which has opened a window to the world, and the possibility to "share" comments, ideas, images, videos… with other social media users.

We should notice, thirdly, that there is an important growth at the human capital level, the population of the Arab countries has nearly tripled since 1970, climbing from 128 million to 359 million. The Arab Region is expected to have 598 million inhabitants by 2050, increasing by two-thirds or 239 million more people than in 2010.[3] There is also an important Urbanisation process in motion and migration from Rural to Urban Area. These changes are characterized by the transitions from traditional farming activities to manufacturing and service sector employment which employs more and more in the job market, especially at the informal sector, and, according to some experts, it account for about 60% of total employment in poor Arab countries.[4] There is also a large number of youth and those in the working ages, and a small number of elderly people; the

[3] Barry Mirkin, Population Levels, Trends and Policies in the Arab Region: Challenges and Opportunities, Arab Human Development Report, Research Paper Series, United Nations Development Programme, Regional Bureau for Arab States. 2010.

paradox here is that there is more and more failure in managing the growing youth population entering the labour market who suffers more than older generations from high unemployment. In the years to come, there is a need for millions of supplementary jobs to supply the need of market job.

In short, the people who revolted are the urban educated Youth. This youth benefited from some un-intended results of modernisation of the Post-independence Arab societies (education and New Technologies), which came to open their eyes, but also to deprive them from decent living and marginalised from decision making. They believed (and still do!) that they could take their destiny into their own hands, and that they could make their own choices by themselves: they are not "minors", as the dictators thought for a long time. This book engages this perspective of enlightenment, and attempts to be another tribute to freedom thinkers, fighters for social and political equality all over the world, as we share first our humanity and persistent aspiration to dignity.

Revolution…by Love, indeed as Rumi said, "Reason is powerless in the expression of Love."

The individual revolutions that these writers are sharing in this book are another proof that nothing can be explained perfectly, that there will always be magical and hidden reasons that made us experience a situation in a certain way. Yet,

---

[4] After the Spring: Economic Transitions in the Arab World, (collective book), Oxford University Press, USA (March 27, 2012), P: 39.

love is undoubtedly always behind the attempt to explain so that others can learn and engage; and it is love that is brings so much joy in sacrifice and so much patience in despair. The writers wish to say, as Nelson Mandela did, that they are "not nervous of love for love is very inspiring." They hope that their humble experiences will inspire readers to commit and engage in their own societies and communities. They hope to empower readers, to offer them and future revolutionaries hopeful, yet still wise, advise: Revolution is a long process of changing a system to another system, young activists should be armed with a strategic vision, defining their goals and principles, practical tools and tactics, patience, and searching peers to share values and cooperate to achieve their goals. Indeed, we hope readers will be inspired by our accounts and experiences and engage in the political world in order to make our world a place to live life, abundantly for all of us, and the generations of women and men who will follow.

The Book Committee

Dala Ghandour
Mohammed Masbah
Emna Ben Yedder

Amal Matar

BAHRAIN

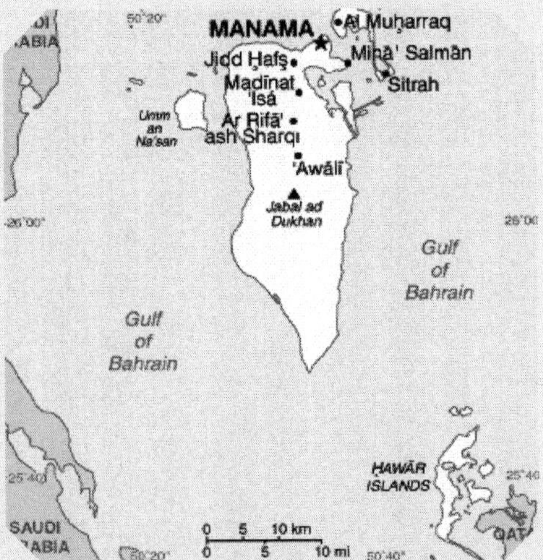

THE PEARL OF THE GULF

The pearl of the gulf, is what Bahrain used to be called. Not only because it is a beautiful small island on the Arabian Gulf that used to depend on pearl industry, but also because its people were well known of their kindness, openness and pureness like a shining pearl. Bahrain was always known of its tolerance and openness to other cultures and religions, and, comparing to other neighboring countries, was advanced in terms of education, civil society and women's rights. It was well known throughout history that all Bahrainis regardless of sect or religion were living in harmony and socializing with each other with mixed marriages, friendships and neighborhoods.

It was a place for many civilizations from the ancient ages. Delmon, Tylus and Awal were some of them. In the 19th century Bahrain was a British Protectorate when Al Khalifa family, who came to Bahrain from the Arabian Peninsula, entered into a treaty relationship with Britain. This treaty granted the Al Khalifa the title of Rulers of Bahrain.

After the independence from Britain in 1971, and based on its new constitution, Bahrainis elected their first National Assembly (Parliament) in 1973. It lasted only for 2 years, and when the authorities faced a serious opposition to some of their plans, the Amir at that time (Sh. Isa Bin Salman Al Khalifa) dissolved the parliament, suspended the related articles in the constitution and announced the States Security Law which allowed the arrest and detention up to 3 years (renewable) without a trial.

This repression—along with other problems related to lack of representation, lack of transparency, corruption, discrimination, unemployment, housing and poverty—led to a popular uprising in 1994 demanding more freedoms and democracy. It was harshly cracked down by the authorities, which killed around 40, detained hundreds and sent many to exile.

The struggle continued until the Amir died and his successor, Sh. Hamad Bin Isa Al Khalifa, came to power. He promised with reforms, released the political detainees and brought back the people from exile. So the people welcomed that and voted for what he announced as the national charter, by 98.4 %, and when he went to visit the villages that were suppressed by the 90s crackdown, the people carried his car – I mean the car wasn't running on the street, it was on the people's shoulders. That explains how the people were happy about his promises to reform.

But soon after that there was a huge disappointment. The promised reforms turned to be only superficial and actually guaranteed the monopoly of power in the hands of the King. The corruption only increased, the discrimination deepened and the unlawful political naturalization added more to the already problematic political situation. The parliament was designed in a way that made it fully controlled by the higher authorities; thus, it could not make any change in terms of combating corruption, holding the officials responsible and improving the living conditions. The poverty, unemployment, housing problems all increased day by day in a country situated amongst the most wealthy oil producing countries.

So Bahrain was boiling and about to explode, and when the Arab Spring started the people were already ready to take to the streets. It was the first Gulf country that responded to the wave of democracy movement. In addition to the above factors, I believe Bahrain was ready also because of another factor, which is education.. It is well known that Bahrainis are highly educated comparing to other neighboring countries and the people that took to the streets were from all educational levels including intellectuals, doctors, lawyers, engineers, atheletes, and from all classes including the middle and high class. So the protesters in Bahrain were not looking for democracy only for a better life in terms of jobs and economy, but also in terms of liberty and dignity.

Being a doctor and working in the only public hospital in Bahrain, I was shocked by the severe brutality of the regime forces against the protesters. The regime harshly cracked down on the protesters, killing more than 80, injuring, detaining hundreds and dismissing thousands from their jobs. The hospital, where I work, was full of casualties on a daily basis, from all different forms of artillery: live ammunition, rubber bullets, shotguns, tear gas and severe beatings.. As an ophthalmologist I was exposed to huge numbers of eye injuries, many of them, unfortunately, lost their eyes. It was estimated that not less than 100 people lost their eyes.

I still remember Jaffar Salman, the 28 year old from Sitra and the father of 2 beautiful young girls, who was shot by shotgun to his face that pierced both of his eyes and rendered him totally blind. The tragedy of Jaffar did not end here, it actually started when the hospital was taken over by military forces, right after GCC troops entered Bahrain to crush the democracy movement.

I was there at the hospital sleeping from the previous night. I remember I shared our small duty room with my colleague because there was not enough rooms for all of us. We were around 6 eye doctors called for duty to deal with the huge number of casualties. So in the morning of 16th March 2011, we woke up on the news of the GCC troops attacking the protesters in the pearl square. As usual, we anticipated a lot of injuries and rushed to the emergency room waiting for the patients to arrive. An hour, or two passed with complete silence and no patient arrived. We looked around us through the windows to see what was going on. We were shocked that the military and security forces were surrounding the hospital and not allowing anyone in or out including the ambulances. A few hours later they entered the parking lot of the hospital until they reached the main door of the ER. We were frightened and looking at them through the windows and watching them clapping and dancing and we were wondering why and what they were up to.

Soon they entered the hospital, masked with guns and took over the administration offices. We thought of leaving the hospital, but through the intercom they ordered us not to leave. We saw some nurses trying to leave, but got caught by police and severely beaten up until they couldn't move. We slept that horrible night at the hospital, terrified of what might happen next and wondering why. The next day we knew why. They arrested doctors from within the hospital and accused them of occupying the hospital and killing the protesters by exaggerating their wounds. Those well known, highly qualified and specialized doctors did nothing but treat the injuries caused by the brutality of the security forces. Some of them used to be my teachers in the medical school and some of them trained me in the hospital. One of them is an ophthalmologist whom I witnessed working day and night to save eyes that were shot by police. One of the doctors, an orthopedic surgeon, was arrested from the operating room while the patient was on the table.

The next day, they started searching for the protesters inside the hospital and identified them from their wounds. They arrested many of them, and collected all who couldn't walk to particular wards, known later as "the torture wards." At night, police used to come interrogate patients and torture them on their beds and force them to give false confessions. When a patient was able to move from bed, they were taken to detention centers.

It was a horrible situation for me to see my colleagues being arrested and my patients taken one by one. I still remember Jaffar, the patient that lost both eyes, begging us to ask the police to let him call his family or let someone visit him. I remember he was worried about his family and who would take care of them. My eyes teared when he said he just wanted to give them his credit card so they could live. But the police had no mercy for this young blind guy who lost his sight and future because of them. I remember the nurses crying from the horrible experiences at night when they would see the police beating up on the patients' wounds.

`Jaffar's tragedy did not end here either. He was taken from the hospital to a detention center, charged with illegal gathering (which simply means protesting), tried before a military court and sentenced to 2 and a half years. He is still in jail as I am writing now. I never heard of him until a year later when a human right activist wrote about him and how he was denied medical care for his eye in prison. I called this activist and got the contact of his family and realized that he was suffering from pain and photophobia and the jail guards did not care to take him to any clinic. His photophobia prevented him from participating in outdoor activities because he could not tolerate the sun light. What a punishment he got for simply rising up and saying he had a voice.

At home, it was not an easier situation at all. After the crackdown on the democracy movement, my husband expected that he would be arrested. He was a member of the parliament and resigned in protest against the regime's brutality. He was outspoken in criticizing the regime and exposing the human rights violations. We lived in terror especially after a false confession was aired on T.V. about my husband by one of the detainees that died in custody under torture. On 2nd May 2011, and while I was with him in the car, we were chased by armed masked men in plain clothes and civilian car. They kidnapped my husband from the street. It was a terrifying moment and I was just praying that they would not assassinate him. From this moment, I did not know anything about him until 3 weeks later when he called just to say he was OK. He was not allowed to say where he was or who was holding him. A month and 10 days later we heard that he was taken to a military court, charged with illegal gathering and distributing false information to disturb the state's security. He was put in solitary confinement, tortured and kept in jail for 3 months and 10 days just to punish him for daring to speak out. It was a very tough time for my family and my 2 young children Ahmed and Sarah. It was very hard for me to explain to them why they could not see their father, and when we finally were allowed to visit

Al Yusuf - When my husband was released

him in jail, it was even more difficult to explain why he was surrounded by police carrying guns and why he couldn't come back home.

When I remember all what we went through, I start to wonder why the authorities had such an aggressive and exaggerated response to relatively simple popular demands. Compared to Tunisia, Egypt, Libya, Yemen and Syria the demands of Bahraini people were simple. They were demanding reforms within the monarchy: the transition from an absolute to a constitutional monarchy where the people are the source of all powers and not the ruling family. Bahrain has the longest serving prime minister on Earth situated on his seat for 42 years now. He is appointed and cannot be changed because he is from the ruling family. 13 ministers cannot be questioned or held accountable because they are all from the ruling family. Large areas of the beach lands are owned by the ruling family and know one can ask why. The Bahrainis have every reason to raise their demands for reforms in the form of elected government, a fairly representative parliament, independent judiciary and inclusive security that reflects all the Bahraini community. The harsh crackdown and regime's brutality, however led some segments of the opposition to call for overthrowing the regime. Still the mainstream opposition are calling for reforms within the regime in the form of the above demands. Unfortunately, all segments of the opposition found nothing but a deaf ear.

Sadly, the Bahraini regime is supported not only by the GCC monarchies, but also largely by its ally, The United States. Bahrain is a strategic non-NATO ally for The United States hosting the U.S fifth fleet. It is very difficult to understand why the most democratic country and advocate for human rights is backing such authoritarian regime with such a bad human rights record. Unfortunately, democracy and human rights don't seem to come first in the foreign policy of The United States. What we see on the ground is that the stability is what really matters. As long as this regime guarantees the interests of The United States in security and oil, any change is considered to be worrisome. In my view, I think that does not only contradict the American values, but also reflects a shortsighted vision. I believe the democratic change is inevitable and the people who are now weak and oppressed will come one day to power and will remember who stood by their side. The U.S. can build bridges with both the people and the regime and can make its ally a more strong and prosperous country through pushing for reforms and respect of human rights.

In contrast to our frustration with the US government, Arab spring was an eye opening experience to the wonderful and dynamic American civil society. We were amazed by the huge support we got from the American democracy and human rights organizations. We were also amazed by the professionalism of the American journalists in covering the events of the uprising. We are very thankful for all our American friends who spoke for us and supported our cause for democracy and stood against the human right abuses in Bahrain. I would like to especially thank Joe Stork from Human Rights Watch, Staci Haag from NDI, Brian Dooley from Human Rights First, Steve McInerney and Cole Bockenfeld from Project of Middle East Democracy and Richard Sollom from Physicians for Human Rights. I cannot forget to thank May Welsh, an American journalist, who put herself at risk during her coverage of the events in Bahrain and produced the great documentary Shouting in the Dark.

My hope is to see the gap between the position of the US non-governmental organizations and the US government decreases, and democracy and human rights to be considered a priority in the US foreign policy by actions and not by words.

Ibrahim Yousif Shebani

LIBYA

LIBYA:
THE REVOLUTION OF FOUR DAYS

"Libya is unlike Egypt and Tunisia" Saif-Elislam Gadafi. A quote awakened many Libyans and made them look deeper into what Libya *really* is. With 2000 KM on the Mediterranean, a population of 6 million, Libya has the 10th-largest proven oil reserves of any country in the world and the 17th-highest petroleum production. These are some of many facts most Libyans never bothered to think about with a monthly income of 150$ per family. Libyans spent more time thinking about how they would provide a decent living to their families—about *why*, with a daily income of 200 million LYD from selling oil, Libya remains one of the world's poorest nations.

Seven months after the beginning of the uprising in Libya, more than 40,000 of Libya's youth went missing, 30,000 were martyred and there were horrific stories of rape and torture circulated around every Libyan household spreading fear and anger.

I woke that 12th day of February to find an invitation on Facebook to join a group calling for an uprising in Libya inspired by the huge success of Egypt and Tunisia's revolutions. *This is a joke*, I thought as I went about randomly inviting friends to join. And some of my friends' reaction was to remove me as a Friend on Facebook. As word of mouth was circulating in Libya, the Facebook page and the possibility of an uprising was the core conversation in every café and gathering in Libya. None expected a major event, and those who did said it most probably would be as big as previous incidents such as the protests Libya went through in 2000 and 2006.

A couple of days passed and as I was talking over the phone to my friends in Benghazi I was advised to be there in case things became serious. At the beginning, I saw no point for traveling to Benghazi but after hearing few of my friends say this would be a historical moment whether or not it succeeds. Just the fact that you can be in the streets in Libya holding up signs asking for reforms in the government was something Libyans never experienced or dreamed to do in Libya before.

At a dear friend's birthday dinner on the 15th of February, I received a phone call from one of my friends, Ahmed, in Benghazi telling me that Benghazi has awakened and a massive protest in front of the security directory started after capturing the Busleem Massacre lawyer. The protest was mainly formed by the mothers, daughters and wives of Busleem massacred prisoners and everybody was chanting, *Wake up! Wake up! Benghazi, the day you have long awaited has come!* Mixed emotions of worries over my friends and family in Benghazi and happiness that dormant people of Libya had taken an action was clear on my face and the birthday dinner become a debate session between pro-peace and anti-Gadhafi viewpoints. There were doubts: Would Libyans overpower Gadhafi? What is going to happen exactly? Each and every one of us couldn't predict what was going to happen but I was certain of only one thing, that to Benghazi I must leave in the morning.

I arrived home from the birthday party and signed onto Facebook where videos of the first protest were uploaded. I couldn't believe what I was seeing. I shared the videos in my Facebook page and received an enormous amount of phone calls from friends telling me to remove the videos. I knew if I got caught I would be facing real troubles but after thinking about it, I concluded that what I was doing wasn't really dangerous, and if the government wanted to abort a revolution they would have so many other things to take care of rather than spying on people's Facebook accounts. Back then, I never thought I would have friend who would take Gadhafi's side, a little naïve I was.

I arrived in Benghazi on the 16th of February on the 8:00 p.m. flight. My friends, Ahmed and Suliman, picked me up from the airport and we went straight to downtown where many young Libyans already started protesting and had clashes with police forces loyal to Gadhafi. We parked the car at one of Benghazi's older alleys called VIA TORINO that was built back in the days of the Italian canalization of Libya. We were a bit far but we could hear people chanting, whistling, and clashing with police forces but yet no killing had started. As we got close to join and see what's happening and walked through the dark alleys of downtown Benghazi, we were warned by the police forces and some armed men. They told us to keep distance or the consequences would be severe. It was the three of us and a few other guys making a group of about ten people that gathered at the corner of the street. Some of the guys didn't care and started to scream and curse Gadhafi. The police started marching slowly towards where we were standing. I wanted to run. It was one of the scariest moments I have been through, but the guys where telling us not to chicken out. All of us started running towards the parked cars as the police forces proceeded holding batons.

It was impossible for us to join the protestors. From this side, we drove the car through the alleys to find a way to join the protestors. Ahmed is a brilliant driver and knows downtown Benghazi like the back of his hand. We parked somewhere next to Jamal Abdul Nasr Street and went down. We were very close to the protestors but yet very scared to join. All I could see was security forces trying clamp down on the protestors and angry protestors shouting, *Down! Down, Gadhafi!* and *The police's duty is to serve and protect the civilians!* and *The people want the downfall of the regime!* This took me by surprise and this boost of adrenaline rushed through my veins. I wanted to join the front line of the protestors and shout many things I dreamed of saying ever since we came back to live in Libya from exile back in the early 90s. I turned on my mobile phone video camera over my head with my hoody and wore the sunglasses I had in my pocket.

I joined the protestors and I couldn't stop screaming, *The people want the downfall of the regime!* As I arrived to the front, I saw security forces blocking the main TREE square and a camera man working for the regime trying to film the protestors. That was one of the Ghadafi regime's dirty games; it only meant that they would pick up these protestors in their homes later. As I was pretty covered up in a hoody, sunglasses and a beard, I figured they would never be able to identify me. Then, all of a sudden, I saw Mr. M.B, who I knew worked for the government. I went to school with his daughter, and his other daughter was one of my sister's best friends and they lived next to my aunt's house. I knew his whole family! I thought, *Why is he doing this? Why is he there to harm the young protestors? Why? Because they are calling for reforms?* As I saw him, I got scared thinking, *What if he recognizes me?* I ran back to join my friends at the end of the street. We decided to leave and as we got close to the car, the security forces started chasing the protestors capturing as many as possible. As they were chasing us, I looked to my right and saw Suliman running next to me. *Where is Ahmed?* I asked our other friend. Ahmed weighs over 110 kilograms and had several operations on both of his legs after a car accident a few years ago. We couldn't find him behind us. We looked. We stopped, but they were getting closer. We started shouting, *Ahmed!* And there he was, actually running faster than both Suliman and me. After what he saw the night before, he was scared of being captured and I guess the adrenaline boost helped him. That was the joke we talked about all night.

The guys dropped me off at my family's house and from the moment I stepped in I couldn't stop talking about what happened to my family. I was happy, proud. I was over the TOP. I even started saying the quotes we said back in the streets at home, "The people want the downfall of the regime!" When I went to my bed that night, all I could think of was what would happen next. *Is it worth it?* I come from a well-off family, lived in a villa, had my own business and car, and often travelled. *Why am I putting myself in the situation?* Yes, I do agree that we live like cattle, we have no rights, no freedom of speech, no freedom of press. The country was messed up, but I always had contacts and knew someone who knew someone to get through all the obstacles of living in Libya.

I woke up early on the 17th of February like a little kid on his way to his first day of school. February 17 is the day all of Benghazi was going out. Although I knew that the protest wouldn't start until 3 p.m. I got ready and waited for my friends to pick me up. Suliman arrived at around 1:30. We drove towards downtown as we were passing on the bridge of Juliana that crosses the lake of Benghazi where there was a massive garden often visited by families. I saw something I didn't understand quite well at that time. The garden was full of workers wearing yellow helmets probably over 1000 workers, clearly immigrants, mostly Africans and some Asians. I looked at Suliman and told him, *This is pretty smart. They brought workers to clean up the mess of the protest to show the world that nothing is happening in Benghazi.*

I had no clue what the regime had in mind for the protestors. We arrived at the court where only around five protestors, mainly lawyers, gathered. There, I was disappointed. According to the vision I structured in my mind, every Libyan in

Benghazi was going to be there. I decided to leave and head back to Tripoli. *This is a joke,* I said. Suliman was kind enough to drive me to the airport and all I was thinking about was how I would spend my Friday in Tripoli, maybe coffee with friends talking about actions from the night I spent in Benghazi, probably working had too may deadlines to take care of and clients waiting! As I was getting close to the airport, my friend Salma called, *Ibrahim are you in front of the court?* she asked. *No, not really*, I responded, *I went and nothing was happening.* She said, *No, man, I just talked to people and they are arriving to the court from every street in Benghazi. Everybody is marching to the court! Even women are going!* I thought a bit about it and asked Suliman, *What do you think? Should we go back?*

We drove back. There weren't many people out in front of the court, but protestors started chanting, *Constitution, freedom and equality!* We joined them waiting for the rest to arrive. Suliman made some phone calls and everybody we called said they were on their way. Thousands of people were marching from downtown Benghazi and through the western part of the city. Others found their way in small groups. We were clearly over 5000 Libyans all in one voice shouting, *Tell Moamer and his sons, Benghazi is full of real men!* and provoking some Libyans who kept watching from a distance, out of fear, encouraging them with a chant, *Join us! Join us and no harm would reach you!*

Our numbers were increasing. I couldn't stop calling family and friends telling them about what I was witnessing. We waited for the marching groups to join us and no one arrived! We received a phone call from our friend, Osama, and he told us his side of the story. Over 10,000 men were marching. He said he went up on a mosque's roof to see the end of the line and he said he could see men marching for as far as he could see. These men went over the bridge crossing the lake of Benghazi and had no clue what was waiting for them including my friend,

Osama. As they were passing the bridge, mercenaries dressed in custodial outfits and yellow helmets were providing support to the army who were shooting at the unarmed protestors with heavy artillery, anti-aircraft weapons, Kalashnikovs, tear bombs, batons, machetes. Chaos broke through. Protestors were being pushed back, and those on the front lines were murdered. Many of them jumped in the lake and many of them were captured. The people gathered in front of the court were receiving phone calls and many stories were being told and anger was showing on the protestors' faces. Everybody was shouting, *People want the downfall of Gadhafi!* I saw rage and anger that nothing could stop and people decided to spend the night in front of the court. We decided to leave by 10 p.m. and head over to see what was happening in front of Alfadel Buomar Brigade Compound which is Gadhafi's most important site of power in Benghazi. We parked a bit far and as we got closer, we could see the military shooting carelessly at groups of young men. We ran. Soon, we found Osama and Mohamed and it was Mohamed's time to tell us his story. He was marching earlier that day with thousands of men through Jamal Abdul Nasser Street. He told us that women were ululating in balconies and sending off their husbands and sons to join the march. Women were chanting, *See how beautiful my country is! Look at the sons of Libya who would die protecting it!* He said that men were marching with tears flowing from their eyes out of pride and joy and the sounds of ululating women would echo everywhere. These marching protestors weren't much luckier. As they approached the court, they were attacked by military and mercenaries/"yellow helmets" the term used by Benghazi people.

On the 18th of February, I woke up early to go with my friend Ahmed to try to collect money, blankets, pillows, mattresses, and food for the crowd that decided to camp in front of the court until the fall of the regime. There were still police and military forces in the streets, and we were trying to find our way through the allies of Benghazi to avoid them. We went knocking door to door and every house we visited didn't hesitate to supply us with everything available. By noon, my friends were all heading to the graveyards to attend the burial of the martyrs who were killed on the previous day. Families and friends of the martyrs started protesting in front of the security directory on the way back from the cemetery.

I was heading downtown and all I could see were big clouds of smoke coming up from most of the regime's buildings. The people of Benghazi were fighting without arms; all they had was gas, matches, rage and will. Security forces were pushed back from downtown towards either the Alfadel Buomar Brigade Compound or to the Security Directory Building. As I approached the court, the only thing I could see was a massive independence flag waving from the court house! This flag was even forbidden to talk about during the past 42 years and the majority of Libyans who were born and raised under the Gadhafi regime didn't even know it existed. In front of the court, there were thousands and thousands of protestors. Many of my friends that I hadn't seen for a while were there, too. The feeling was indescribable. As I was standing and chatting with some of my friends, I saw Mohamed Nabous. He told me he was going home to bring a satellite Internet system to the court in order to connect to AlJazeera. He wanted to go live on the air to show the world what was really happening in front of the court of Benghazi. At that time, no proper videos were broadcasted, only some amateur camera phone videos. He was trying to find other people to come with him to carry the satellite Internet. We got into a pickup truck. He sat in the front with the driver, and I sat in the back with these two guys that I never met before. One of them was named Ahmed Barassi and the other was this creepy guy who acted so weird. He did not stop talking, and at one point he was asking us for our names, addresses, and phone numbers. I learned that Ahmed Barassi was the nephew of someone I knew, so I felt better that I could trust Ahmed. We started speaking in English for the other guy not to understand us. We agreed that this other man was suspicious and concluded he must be one of Gadhafi's spies. Ahmed decided to call Mohamed Nabous who was sitting in the front to tell him about our doubts. After all, the city is still controlled by Gadhafi and it will not be in Mohamed's advantage if Gadhafi's people found his house. We decided to drop off the weird guy about 30 kilometres away from Mohamed's house and told him to wait there and we went to bring the satellite.

It took almost 45 minutes to move the heavy satellite dish, and this time I sat in the front with the driver and the other guys went in another car. All I could see at that time was a helicopter. It was flying over Mohamed's house, and I was concerned they were taking pictures from that helicopter. I thought, *What if they have a machine gun over there?* As we were driving and getting closer to the court, I was trying to calm myself down, but couldn't help but worry, *What if we were stopped by the police or the army?* I told the driver to let me do the talking if we were stopped. We made up a story together and decided we would tell them that this satellite we were carrying was just a normal TV satellite dish and that we are making a delivery. I would tell them I was a technician. After all, they wouldn't be able to distinguish an Internet satellite dish from a TV satellite dish. *How would they know?* As we were getting closer the city, the streets were empty, and the only thing we could see was the smoke of the burning buildings. We arrived safely to the court. That was my mission of the day. People were happy to see the satellite. Finally, the world would witness our happiness, our liberation. I felt so proud to be part of this small mission.

Dala Ghandour

LEBANON

THE HEART REVOLUTION

"Memory is the fabric of identity." Nelson Mandela

I was blessed to be born in a loving family that taught me the beauty of values, knowledge and freedom. I can't keep these gifts of life just for me; I want to share with others the possibility of building a society that believes in the wealth of diversity, the strength of knowing one's own identity and living it in peace with others.

"Independent and you?"

I've always had a curious glance to and at the world; I am always trying to understand it, to know more about a certain situation, and analyze things. I see myself as Alice in Wonderland, the world being a wonder and myself an actor in a film with chapters, stories, and anecdotes. For me, the supreme intelligence is to connect and link the events I lived, the people I met, with an invisible line; and the person who incarnates best this philosophy of life is my grand-father. I can't stress and express enough the impact of his influence in my life. He is one of the best persons I have known

My grand-father, Hekmat Kassir. "If you see someone in need, give him half of what you have, God will reward you always. He is the Most Generous."

in my life, my role model, and my love for him grows every day, because I see that what he stands for is unique. He still impresses me with his humanity and openness to all religions; he is a school by itself.

In Paris, I use to spend hours and hours with my grandfather "Jeddo", watching the news, reading *Le Monde* (French newspaper meaning "The World" and I was truly discovering the world!) two to three hours every night, he had the answers to all my questions: Brazil or Alaska, just choose any topic. My grand-father is the real example of a generation that started work early but never stopped learning; to this day he takes courses in history at 90 years old. My questions were: "Jeddo, explain to me what's really happening here, what are the causes of this strike, how do you think that we can improve this?" He built my critical thinking and what I liked the most about him is that he was always defending the poorest and suggesting options to make their life easier, far from any sectarian, racial considerations. We had these wonderful, passionate, endless conversations that are still ongoing in my mind to this day. I learned so much from him: I learned integrity, history, economics, how to be a better human being. And most importantly, his life and daily actions reflected his thoughts and values: he walked the talk all the way.

Here lies the importance of creativity and power of youth. An idea has a starting point but we never know where it can lead us. I definitely know from where my interest in public field, in politics, my love for my country comes from but I would never have imagined that an idea would have taken me so far.

I was born 32 years ago, in 1981, in the capital of a small special country situated between Syria and occupied Palestine: Lebanon. Lebanon is like that young/old middle aged man, who has lived many lives, been wounded many times and still finds the strength to be tender... And I just have one wish: I wish to sit next to him and see him continue to grow by the sea with wisdom and craziness, for the next century! This is my own metaphor for a Lebanon that has so many images in other imaginations. Each citizen has his allegory of a nation and tries to revive it in his own way. My Lebanon was shaped by people around me who were role models in their daily life.

In Lebanon, where we have 18 communities, diversity could be beautiful if we are truly raised to believe in it. I was blessed. I grew up in an environment where all different kinds of festivities were celebrated and understood; where friends of my family from all backgrounds laughed, discussed, agreed on issues regarding life, politics, etc. I was blessed to learn that the sectarian barriers being built every day are not true. The image of being one in many and many in one is beautifully symbolized with nature, the fig which holds so

"The Ghandour Love"

"The special bond that makes me love my country" with my lovely cousins and sister!

many colors and still is a strong unit, and the pomegranate that is big and rich because of each grain in it. We have so many lessons to learn from nature…I am an ardent defender of knowing truly your identity and always going to the "other" who is another you, in a different mirror. When talking about different dialogues of cultures and religions, I am convinced that this attitude of being open cannot be learned overnight, or in a single conference; rather *openness is a lifestyle* that shows you how important it is to respect yourself and the views of others. The goal of such a lifestyle is not to convert anyone but rather to value the beauty of knowing thus understanding a person, which does not necessarily mean that you agree with her/him all the time and about every issue.

Beirut, my city, taught me that. It has always been a treasure dear to my heart. Here, you are taken by the sounds, horns, smells, colors of a small city that have seen so much and still stands strong and alive like the Phoenix… For me although the architecture is not typical of an Arab city, it has its heart. It has always been open to everyone from all nationalities: refugees, oppressed, exiles, artists who would write, create and print books here. Openness, diversity, friendliness, this is the Beirut I know and that I want to preserve, see develop and thrive. This special vibe and scent is precious and when I see that some are trying to categorize it, label it, imprison it under one color , one community, one identity , I get angry.

Thus, from all of the above, I was always interested in changing the world and making it a better place, and I participated in many events. Until the day where my call of life arrived, April 2010: I decided to run for the municipality elections as an independent candidate with a program, doing my own campaign with one aim to empower the citizens, especially youth, about their voice in civil society. This goal and passion did not leave me since. It brought me so much confidence and assertiveness that changes will come, it is only a matter of time: *we are actors in the process of doing the history of nations.*

There are moments that determine a lifetime; a turning point that you know you should do, if not you will regret it all your life. This is how I felt on this Saturday 24 April 2010, when I registered myself as an independent candidate for Beirut municipality elections. I was afraid, anxious and hesitant, still I knew deep down inside that I would betray the essence of myself if I did not do it. The notary could not believe me. He was deeply convinced that I was on someone else's agenda, and I was sad to see that people could only see a bipolar world, in two colors: with us or against us, although it is freedom that defines us.

Ultimatums always frighten me: they narrow freedoms when we have the luxury to have it all; ultimatums so easily erase nuances and complexities of a fascinating world. The sad reality was that candidates were lining up on the lists waiting to be chosen by parties, as if they were submitting CVs. Serving a country is more than that, we are asking for the trust of constituents not a guarantee to win. My award was the respect of my citizens and their efforts to reach out to their own networks, this was my pride. My 10-days campaign was successful because these citizens participated in it and considered it as a *personal* cause. They spread the word, from Lebanon and overseas, by all means: messages, mails, Facebook status or profile pic, word of mouth, attaching my campaign poster on cars and personal shops… Because of them, I had 1, 470 votes and I was ranked number 7 among 75 candidates who were not elected.

Still, when making the decision I felt weak and strong at the same time. I cried at my friend's boutique but she found the right words to say, simple words of friendship and love. All that I needed to hear… You would be amazed where support can lead you: it is not poetry, it is not just words. I *lived* it with random people in Beirut streets: they would be so proud and supportive of new faces in politics. As they liked to say about me, "We need new blood", offering to help me with ideas, distributing pamphlets after Friday's prayer or on the day of the elections. No one told me that I was too young (I was 29 and looked 24!) or that a woman's place is in the kitchen, resisting all the stereotypical lines that would have prevented me to run. The enthusiasm and kindness of my compatriots gave me the strength to carry on my mission as I saw their unwavering hope; and no one could convince me now that the power of change is not there.

The power of change is there, people just don't know the power of their voices, how they can inspire, challenge the status-quo and the social-economical conventions. I will never forget this guy who was verifying ballots for a major party, and he told me something that touched me "I saw you on TV doing your campaign, and you touched my heart: I couldn't not put your name on the list." I felt so blessed that he could see how sincere I was, the love beyond the act, and I said to myself, if I touched his heart then there are a lot of people who I could move too. People are amazing. It's so sad that we are prisoners and victims of sectarianism: Lebanese people are not tough or brutal, they love

"Aunty" Sahar Sammakie Anouti (RIP) , your support was unconditional and so sincere: I will always remember how you made me feel...

My uncle, Abdo Kassir. " Always search for the answers to your question...by yourself."

My uncle, Maher Kassir. "You can do whatever you want, I believe in you." Always so supportive...

life, music, dance but you cannot imagine how sectarianism can influence them and how they can go against their own interests totally blinded by tribalism and fear.

Yasmine Kaidbey & Kevork Baboyan , your support on this sunny Sunday and enthusiasm gave me so much strength and happiness. You were distributing my program and talking about it as yours, Thank You!

For me, my candidacy was a victory and the best thing I have ever done in my life! I grew up in confidence, with achievements, trust in my dreams and I simply grew up because people were giving me, with their voices, more responsibility as a young woman in society. They believed in my ideas, it is so powerful and amazingly beautiful to me…

It was not easy; it was not fun to expose myself to the "political scene," and to reveal myself with no previous experience in this field. Since my early childhood, I had always been very shy and, what we call, an "intellectual" girl who would observe the world, listen to others and hardly talk. I used to spend all my free time reading books and novels, which enabled me to live different lives and characters, in this magical way proper to books. My best friends were Anna Karenina, The Three Musketeers, Monte Cristo, Les Miserables, Phedre, Antigone; characters I used to identify with and passionately enter in their world. It is not surprising that my school friends when they first saw my campaign poster on Facebook thought I was joking. It is remarkable how a person can still be the same and totally change her attitude to life; for me it was being lighter that saved me from sinking into my own self; a decision I took when I turned 15.

The decision of running tackled me 6 months before the elections and I was asking myself (and my mother!) every single day, first thing in the morning and last thing in the night, if I should go for it or not. My mother's answer every day was the same: you don't belong to this world, it is a dirty one with sharks all over. And my response to her every day was: If I don't do it, who will? If change does not start with me then it will never start for me, as I truly believe that it would make a difference in my being. I used to consult random people about this decision till the last two weeks before running.

My mother, Fadia Kassir. "Knowledge is always yours and no one can take it from you".

One of the memorable ones, in this last period, was a conversation I had with a schoolmate who I bumped into at a restaurant. I was so stressed that I was red and had blotches. I was feeling horrible, so I said to myself, if I don't do it I will die, I will die, physically and psychologically. I told her, "I'm thinking of being a candidate, what do you think?" She said, "No, wait till you are a certified lawyer, when you will have a name in society, status. You know people will expect this and want someone like that to represent them in society." She was saying this and I was saying, "Yes, maybe you are right." She told me, "You don't want some people to mock you or ridicule you...?" I came back home with her thoughts, but my inner voice was stronger; it kept saying, *go go go, no matter what.* I saw her a week later, and I had taken the position to run all the way, so she told me, "Dala, I want to speak to you. I'm sorry about what I said the other day. I wanted to send you a message to let you know to please run, you should do it. You have everything needed for the position, the people who are there are not better than you." I told her that I had taken the decision already.

This mindset is common in the Arab world: it is all about your value in society, your name and reputation. We care about what others have to say about us: your actions and looks are always under strict scrutiny. And what if you run and then lose? Your pride and dignity would not allow it. People would perceive it in a certain way; they would see it as black and white: winning or losing the battle, if not the entire war! They would not think that you are running for something higher, for your own passion of a city, of a country, and that this is a victory in itself to stand up for what you believe in. They probably did not have the blessing of having a grand-father who told them that speaking up for yourself is the most important thing, that even if you only get one voice (my own!), it is worth the trial, you would have accomplished your mission.

Do you know the luxury of having parents telling you we think so and so about your decision, but if you really want to do it, try it? How precious. I have never been given a greater lesson for freedom, a better lesson for democracy than what was practiced in my own house. Here lies the power and importance of education: what we learn by listening cannot compete with what we learn by living. You can have different ideas and opinions and still talk about it, you have a say, a place, a space. This is why I was never really used to ask for authorization from my

"The Complicity", thank you Jeddo for being the best grand-father, friend and teacher in the world...

father to do something, why I would go and ask from a particular leader to be on his list, knowing that if you are on the list then you abide by all the rules of the so called "party." In Lebanon we don't have ideological parties; it is more about sectarian parties protecting their people as we are living a deficiency of citizenship. The State is so weak that it cannot protect its own people, so they turn to a one-man show leader who will promise them to recruit their sons, pay for the medication of their mothers and, by doing this, win their belongings forever! Clientelism can only sustain itself by avoiding the building of strong and transparent institutions.

My parents. "Be what you want to be, we will always support you." Forever Grateful...

Unfortunately, many of the candidates for political offices run for obvious personal interests. I could feel how citizens are turned into subjects, and, more importantly, how citizens turn to people who just want their own benefits. If you really want to

My father, Misbah Ghandour.
"Here is my country and family, nothing can change that, I am staying."

make a change in your country *you go and do it*, you don't ask someone if they will be kind enough to take you on their list. But there is more to it than this. This really embittered me because I said to myself, if we continue the "pseudo-democracy" (before the Arab Spring) that Lebanon is, then very soon we will be a dictatorship. In this democracy, we can say whatever we want. You can run for whatever campaign you want, so we have a certain freedom at least; and this precious freedom is being taken from the people by their own selves. The most dangerous thing is that people who were maybe ready, who had a program, who had a vision for their city, censored themselves because they said, "We don't want to go against X party, it would be not well viewed because we are from the same religious community so it would be dangerous for us, our interests or the interests of our families..."

I learned one important thing: people respect courage and a normal citizen will lead when convinced by what s/he does. My victory was when I could empower a citizen to vote, and if this citizen was not convinced to vote for my program, to vote blank. We owe it to Beirut to give up some of our free time on election days; after all, "bad officials are elected by good citizens who do not vote" (Nathan).

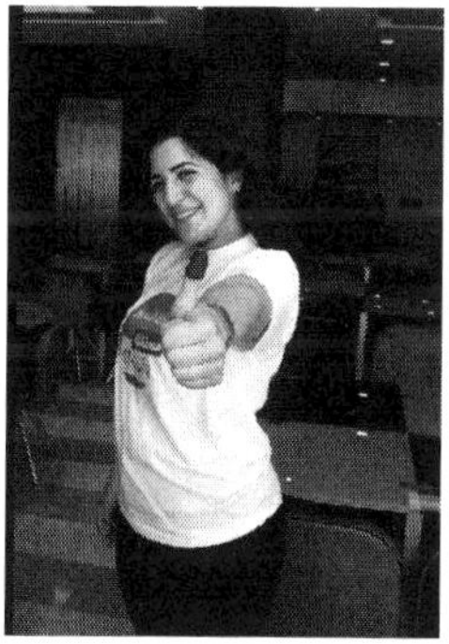

Participate. "Your vote is your voice." Use it !

It is no wonder that when I was sharing my program on the streets, some people were totally surprised by what I was doing because they have only known "bad officials" who used them, who made their lives unbearable with frequent lies, crazy real estate prices and a gap between the rich and poor that is getting higher every day. I didn't take it personally, because for me, it's because we are silent and not positively active in our community that we are allowing such politicians to rule us. This will only change when we consider that politics is part of our daily life and that we have a responsibility to give choices to voters, to make our politicians accountable for their actions and promises. This will only change when we express our thoughts, even if there are no followers: be convinced and others will follow!

For me it was simple. I was not going to vote for people whose only merit was that they were on the winning list because they were chosen by the politically correct party in the city; this decision not taking into consideration what they will offer the city during the next 6 years. So I wrote my program and spread it via social media.

The core of my program evolved around preserving heritage, identity and passing it on to the youth. I deeply believe that when you know where you are coming from you are richer and you reach out for others with ease and confidence.

I am truly shaken when I see an old house being destroyed to have another skyscraper taking its place, because history gives its soul and shape to a city. I am particularly sad when I see people passing everyday by Beirut streets and their names, not knowing why these streets have these names and the origins, not even having the curiosity to know who the person is that their house street is named after. War turned us into a short memory city, where everything is consumed quickly, burnt out without having the time to reflect upon it. As you never know what your tomorrow will be about, with frequent incidents happening all over the country, you might as well enjoy your day and not worry about anything but your little pleasures of life. It is the beauty and the curse of the people of this country: they forget too quickly when they should remember the past so it won't continue to haunt them. Lebanon is wounded by 15 years of civil war with horrible crimes against humanities based on nationality, religion and deeply disturbed people survived these events: *we still have a lot of wounds of history that need to be healed.* By spreading mediation and disrupting geographical stereotypes, one would contribute to bring people together. Because we still have people who are not going to other regions or districts, because they are still afraid of the other, and fear can take you very far with hatred and destruction. Beirut could be this role model city as it hosts all colors, religions and thoughts. The municipality could do a great job in bringing people together, and it would be a base to have the capital city and to build a better citizen, that would be a positive spiral for the country. It is essential for all citizens to consider and know the power of her/his voice, and the responsibility s/he holds with this voice. My aim was to raise awareness in the society about the importance of knowing who is representing you; I wanted to make the people aware that whoever we choose to represent us has an impact on our direct life, and also that we have a role, a duty to not keep our mouths shut, and to work with each other. A lot of people came to see me and tell me how brave and courageous my decision to run was. Personally I saw it as something natural and not that complicated. When you are sincere the whole world helps you: people would mention me to their inner circles, on TV, being very excited for me and waiting for the results with impatience. I want to talk about these people whose support was so precious, whose love was a treasure: I gain so much from knowing that we think alike. I just could not remain silent anymore in the name of all what happened and is happening in Lebanon and the region. We cannot keep complaining and change nothing about our own selves; this policy proved us wrong and we paid the price very high.

Silence is not golden, despite what we like to say in our countries; it is remaining silent when we are really shouting on the inside for a better tomorrow that kills us. In my own modest way, I wanted to wake up all the Beirutis with a conscience, who refuse to consider themselves as part of a sect before being part of a nation.

I know that I did inspire my fellow citizens: young or old, women or men. I feel so humbled when someone tells me that s/he just put my name when s/he could have put 23 other names to fill the municipality seats, or that another young woman wants to be a candidate as well one day like me! You can imagine how strong these statements are, they gave me goose bumps and told me how important it truly is to believe in your own self.

At Makassed School, rewarding high school students who wrote about what they would do in their city, if they were the Mayor! They give me hope...

All these silent voices who think they are so weak, who think they are so lonely all over Lebanon, should try at least once to be on the other side and know how powerful and liberating it is. One thing is for sure, those who go to the other side and break the silence will never refrain from speaking again, they will never go back to the initial position, because when you break the barriers that are only created to stop you from dreaming of a better future, you would know that the real "Arab Spring" can only happen if "You" experience it.

Mine started in April 2010 and since then I continue to blossom.

Samah Elmeri

LIBYA

HERE COMES THE REVOLUTION...

Introduction

For a very long time Libya has been portrayed in a negative way, be it internationally or even in the region amongst other Arab countries surrounding it, and that's mainly because of Gaddafi who ruled Libya for 42 years. For me, living under his rule meant to survive in the jungle, a jungle he thought he owned and that we struggled to call *home*. He was present in every corner of the country. There was no voice heard but his voice. There could be no accomplishments but his accomplishments.

To the world, Gaddafi was a brutal dictator; to the Libyans, he was the number one enemy and the reason that the world put Libyans under so much scrutiny. He was the reason we were rarely welcomed in the international community. In the eyes of the world, Libya just meant Gaddafi and nothing else. In my travels, in my years in school away from Libya, and even in those moments when I met new people, I would say, "I'm Libyan" and automatically people's initial reaction would be "Oh, Gaddafi." That's actually when they are able to place it on a map. More often the reaction would be just plain obliviousness.
Libyans lived in the same way other nations went about their days with the exception of the despairing look you would see on peoples' faces. Gaddafi was

barely the issue especially in the recent years, people had gotten used to his big posters all over the country and started to forget the name of their own country and instead called it, "Aljamahiriya", a made up term to signify his thoughts, his strong grip on the country and narcissistic ideologies. People just stopped noticing how bad they had it because they were struggling so much with the basic needs. Libyans learned to survive under Gaddafi because those were the rules to be able to live on Libyan soil. In a very short time, Libya became as miserable as his visions.

Today, Libyans have 30,000 martyrs to thank for the changed image of my beloved Libya.

The Revolution

My family and I were still in Libya at the start of the revolution. We were closely following the events unfolding in both Tunisia and Egypt. It gave us hope. We thought that Libya might take the same path towards a peaceful revolution. As always, Gaddafi had something to say about everything. And when the Tunisian revolution took place and Ben-Ali was ousted, he came out to say that the Tunisian revolution was a grave mistake and that the Tunisians will regret it. He said no one was good enough to be able to rule Tunisia like Ben Ali. To our surprise, however, Gaddafi had nothing to say when the Egyptian revolution began. That's when we realized that he was beginning to worry about Libya. That's when Libyans of all ages, genders and affiliations began to prepare for their own story of a true revolution to unfold in the quest to save the last bits of "true" Libya from Gaddafi.

I remember the first week of the revolution; the English Prime Minister was on television saying that Gaddafi had fled to Venezuela. People came out of their houses cheering and crying, "God is Great." There were fireworks. They really believed it. They thought that he was gone. I told my brother right away, "This is a lie. There's no way Gaddafi would leave the fight. He is not Hosni Mubarak and he is not Ben-Ali. No way in hell. He is someone who would rather kill six million Libyans than leave like his Tunisian and Egyptian fellow dictators. It's all about his pride." At that time, I remember my brother constantly reminding me that Gaddafi would eventually leave or, better yet, die. Eventually, Libya and Libyans would be able to choose their own destiny. My brother's engineering background gave him different way of looking at disasters, especially when it came to his analysis on why Gaddafi's days were much shorter than those of Mubarak or Ben-Ali. He would say that because "Gaddafi took longer years in being a ruler, that the revolution against his rule would be much shorter."

Soon we started to hear rumors of African mercenaries roaming the streets. Their job was to also force men out of their houses to fight. They did that by using the women of the household. They raped them to get the men to go fight. Tripoli had become a war zone overnight. Unfamiliar looking men would shoot into the air to try and intimidate observers. Gaddafi's supporters were taking control over Tripoli. It slowly became unbearable to go through the long hours of the day, always anticipating the worse to come. I had only started my new job and four days into it, I had to stop going. My older sister was pregnant. This added more pressure on my parents and her husband to start preparing for our departure before things got worse.

My father is the barometer of my life. When I see a smile on his face, I know things will be okay. During those heavy time, however, when I looked at him, I would see him worried, distant and in a state of disarray. He knew somehow it was not going to be like the Egyptian revolution or the Tunisian revolution. He knew it would be much worse. That Libyans would have to pay a bigger price.

It was then my father suggested that we leave the country. At least, he said, for "a few days and I will then join you." This was the last thing he said before we left. On the 25th of February, almost a week into the revolution, before the UN "No Fly" zone resolution stopped all air traffic, my father and brother drove us to the airport and from there we left to Cairo thinking it would only be for a few weeks. Instead we were there for eight months.

My father and my brother remained in Libya throughout the revolution. They endured tough times for six months. The regime's grip on Tripoli tightened. They started with electricity being cut-offs. Then the Internet was permanently shut down making communication between us a hassle. We couldn't say much over the phone because they were watching and listening to everything. Food was becoming expensive as well as scarce. Banks ran out of money and became dysfunctional, making their lives an unpredicted mess. They didn't have a lot of cash available and they couldn't go and get any out of the bank. Whatever they had at home was all they could spend. Our biggest worry was that my brother would be forced to join the regime's army since he was twenty-eight years old, which was the target age of men for the army. Our life away from my father, brother and our home was unimaginable. Although we were away from the danger, we worried my pregnant sister was not too strong to handle the daily news and shocks that unfolded by the minute. At times I wished I were physically present in the front lines, because worrying about all of them was unbearable enough.

Yet, I also remember throughout the revolution when we talked to my father, we would be the ones depressed and pessimistic about the situation. He would be the one making jokes to try and make us feel better. Although he was living under the shelling of NATO, the unpredictability of Gaddafi's actions, and the distance forced upon us, he always made us feel that he could handle anything and that it wasn't as bad as we see it in the news. "We're just going to go through it. At the end of the day, whatever God has written for us to see we will see, but we'll have to pray through it." Luckily, this is exactly what got us through it.

The journey back to Libya

We began our journey back to Tripoli on October 4th. At that time Gaddafi had not been captured yet, which was why my father was hesitant at first; however, not having seen him for eight long months, for us, it was worth risking the trip. We believed Tripoli would be liberated. Operation Mermaid Dawn, the name chosen for the liberation mission of Tripoli, was planned for the 20th of the holy month of Ramadan, which added to the significance of the event and the emotional rollercoaster that it brought with it. I remember Libyans all over the world were fasting, praying, and above all believing that God was guiding them through this revolution. We knew that the worst part was over and we had faith that we would be safe. Our plane from Egypt landed in Djerba, Tunisia where we met our uncle, who drove us eight hours straight to our beloved Libya.

On the way back into Libya, I could see the changes in the atmosphere. People were still tense and cautious, but they also seemed relieved and hopeful. They cheered us with "God is Great." They waved the truc and newly proclaimed flag of Libya. You would see the flag on walls, on rooftops and on every checkpoint. Libya finally bloomed with the colors of independence, freedom, and integrity.

Before the revolution, I've always felt suffocated whenever I came back to Libya because as much as I loved my country, I always felt that we were only temporary visitors. It seemed the country was actually owned by one family to rule, abuse, and do as they please. Living in Libya was more like surviving. I had to be creative when it came to looking for means of entertainment, as we had no cinemas, malls nor proper sports arenas like you would imagine, especially that we are considered an oil producing country, hence a wealthy one!

Being a young woman in Libya came with a set of rules of do's and don'ts because Libya generally was a place that caters to Gaddafi loyalists. What I noticed about post-revolution Libyan women taught me a lot more about how Gaddafi had control of the cultural context of the country. I say that because women started contributing more to Libya since the revolution, more than ever before. Today, you can see Libyan women engaging in politics, working hand in hand with men in civil society organizations, and travelling around the world on missions to represent Libya voluntarily. They are doing this work because of their qualifications, not because they are related to the current regime. In the past, women feared becoming a vital part of the community in the previous regime because they knew that any type of attention on them would not bring any good to them or their families. Nowadays however, that is no longer the case.

I was back at work in late October. I came back to Libya with a sense of wanting to give back and knowing that every little effort would go a long way. I wanted to contribute starting with adjusting and adapting to a post-war country, which was surprisingly a smooth experience for most of us. Libya finally has a chance to bloom, prosper and be the beautiful country with the most caring, giving and generous people I know. Even when I complain and nag about the little things that bother me about life in Libya, I know deep down that I am lucky and proud to have been born Libyan.

I remember when we arrived to our neighborhood in the early afternoon. I could not hold the tears at the thought of being alive and home at last. The air felt so enticing reminding me of both the best and worst times of my life. I remember seeing my father open the door before my uncle could brake to stop the car, my sister and I ran out to get our long waited for hugs and kisses from our backbone, rock and hero. *Thank God* is all I said to him; it will be a day I will forever cherish.

Now that Gaddafi's gone...

In the post-Gaddafi Libya, I cannot simply say that life is peaceful and harmonic. I can say that at least Libyans have gained back their dignity and that in itself is an achievement, one that took over forty-two years. During his first speech in response to the Benghazi events, he was adamant, calling all the protestors *"bunch of dirty rats on hallucination pills."* That was only the beginning. His determination and cold bloodedness became obvious to the world and finally showed them the monster we for so long endured. The Libyan revolution was not calling for just a better way of life, better education and job opportunities. It was a national call to regain their sense of pride, dignity and sense of belonging to Libya. Libyans tried in all means to tell the world that Libya belonged to the people, rather than to a lunatic self made leader who thought he was the sole commander of the country and its people.

Now, in a sense, I can walk just a little bit more straight. When I say I'm Libyan, I know that it resonates differently in peoples' minds. It is no longer followed by, "Oh, Gaddafi..." I would like to think that it now at least gives a different vibe and shows that Libyans have always been misrepresented, over shadowed and oppressed in every sense of the word.

On a lighter note, Libyans, just like all the Arabs at the time, were trying to go through the bloody war by making jokes to boost the moral. One very popular joke was comparing the different chants that were invented for each revolution of the Arab spring. We were critiqued for being the last to revolt especially since we had the longest standing dictator and, in my opinion, the most dangerous and evil one of all. In all the other revolutions, the people were loudly demanding their dictators to *"leave."* Libyans were the only ones who bluntly told our bloody dictator that, *"We are coming after you! We will never surrender. We win or we die."* These were the words of the one true Libyan hero, Omar Almukhtar, the grandfather of the freedom fighters.

Today, the situation in Libya is much more complicated, yet still uplifting and inspirational. This is especially true because now difference of opinions are appreciated and respected. There is no longer one opinion, one voice nor one ruler. Now everybody has the right to talk, everybody has an opinion, everybody belongs to Libya, and everybody wants to see Libya in their own way. As much as this brings about a lot of uncertainty and possible chaos, it is expected and accepted by Libyans. We all know now that it is not just Gaddafi we needed to get rid of, but a cultural, intellectual and pragmatic influence that lasted for forty-two years and we are fighting against, on a daily basis. It is so heartwarming to see Libyans from all over the world coming back to Libya for the first time in over thirty years to help in the rebuilding process of their long denied country of birth. It makes me think how thankful I am to always have had access to Libya and how much there is to learn about the history of a country I call home yet I still have to discover. Today more than ever before, I am looking forward to the stories I will one day be telling my revolution-baby-born nephew, Mahmoud.

My Libya.

As a young Libyan, I have been privileged to have experienced and lived through the revolution because it has given women my age a pathway of opportunities to shine and show a side of Libya that very few people outside knew existed. I have been extremely proud to see so many women take part in the political scene as well as in the frontlines when liberating Libya was the task in hand. This in so many ways would help encourage other young women to participate in every other field. I cannot say that it is because of the revolution that Libyan women are keener to participate and engage, however, it has helped them realize that they have an equal share in their own country as the men of Libya do. Women today are becoming more persistent to stand up for anyone who would take that right they fought alongside freedom fighters for.

In the past year, my relationship with Libya has tremendously changed. Living in Libya has always been a challenge for me mainly because of how the country was under-developed or destroyed, psychologically and materialistically. I have begun to finally find reasons to look beyond all that and learn to discover the beauty in it. I try to adapt to the tough changes that Libya is going through. I try to look at the bright side of the picture. I feel the warmth of Libya in my heart. I know that one day my children will be born proud Libyans.

The price paid for me to be able to write these few words without living in fear was a very expensive one that I will eternally treasure and hold as a badge of honor. I've always compared Libya to neighboring countries and used to feel disappointment and an inner anger because Libya seemed to always lose its spark in these comparisons. Understanding what Libya had to undergo, I now respect its uniqueness. I see the incredible mission Libyans have gone through to make it to where we are today.

Shatha Al-Harazi

YEMEN

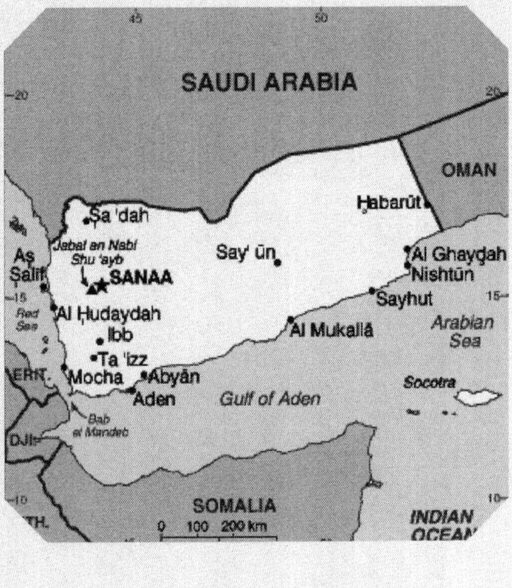

CRAZY GIRLS:
WHAT EVERY REVOLUTION NEEDS

On February 3rd, Yemenis decided to show their rage peacefully. They organized themselves and went out protesting in front of Sana'a University. I had a hard conversation the day before trying to convince my parents that I have to participate to report it to the world. I had to promise my father that I will not leave the house the next morning and join the protest. Everyone was scared to let his family participate as no one knew what the regime's reaction would be. I was told that women were not allowed to participate in the first protest, but I made my mind to go even though I promised not to. The fear of the regime's thugs is huger when it comes to women. I thought carefully and decided that this is a one-time opportunity, if I thought my participation won't make a difference then I don't really believe in the power of change. Also if I believe that my participation would make a difference but someone else could play that role instead of me, then I allow the others to draw the future of my country and to isolate me later on from this process. I was conscious to the result of caring much about my own safety at the time. I decided to go and I contacted two of my female friends who at the beginning wanted to prevent me from going but I convinced them to join.

At the protest sight there were massive numbers of men standing in the streets around Sana'a University. Some of them formed security committees to protect the protesters and we "the three girls" had to convince each committee that our participation as females is as important as theirs.

I felt part of something bigger that is what I can ever recall from that moment of protesting. I finally felt the sense of belonging. The collective call that Yemenis deserve to live equally as any other human being in the world found its way to my heart.

I have always been confused about my identity because I never understood how a person could be told where he or she should belong to just because his father was born in certain country or some people decided to divide the earth in a certain geographical ways. What makes me a Yemeni? I have always questioned this in my head. It's the biggest conflict on earth when you are deeply lost and don't know what makes you who you are, or who you were told to be. The revolution finally gave me an answer on February 3, 2011.

Why Yemenis did go to the streets and never left the protest sight unlike the Egyptians, Tunisians, Libyans or Syrians? However they got the least media coverage or were rarely covered by the mainstream media.

Most media outlets were interested in shaping the general perspective on Yemen through terrorism issues. This is the excitement of covering this type of news. As a reporter and a freelancer, I know by heart if I propose a story on Al-Qeada it will be published, but if I am coving other types of humanitarian stories, I need to put more effort into convincing the editor to publish it.

It's a call for dignity rather for freedom or democracy. Dignity means justice. Yemen is the poorest country in the Middle East with an estimate of 24 million people, and around 40 percent of the population lives under the poverty line.

31.5% of the population lack to food security, and we can hardly say there is a middle class in Yemen. This could be one reason why the revolution in Yemen was not as popular as we wanted it to be; the average individual income in Yemen is less than 2 US Dollars a day. It is a country where one can find a University teacher—which is supposed to be the most respected job—working as a taxi driver after his working hours in the university to economically survive. One of the cases that once made headlines in 2010 was when the Saudi authorities in the borders between Yemen and Saudi burnt some smuggling Yemenis alive. These people were just like others trying to find life in neighboring countries. Youth would only see the hope of survival in taking this huge risk to illegal immigrate. It is all political, and the difficulties and challenges Yemenis face every day is due to the countries administration corruption. Protests are not new in Yemen, and there is always something to complain about and to protest about. People have had in reforms in the last seven years, but having their hopes neglected made them lose it. So they try to get rid of the problems root by toppling the regime. The Journalist's syndicate has been protesting constantly since 2007. There is always violence to protest against and someone to defend. In 2009, a local TV channel reported on a man who killed his seven kids and then himself as a result of poverty. All these stories are reasons that motivated us to protest, to build the hope within ourselves that things will change for the better if we changed the corrupt regime. The youth who protested knew that the country's problems—whether ecumenical or political or social—are all politically driven. And if we changed the regime things will be better.

A book called *Jewel in the Hand of a Collier* by author Turkey Al-Dakhil, describes the different resources of Yemen and the mismanagement and misusage by its administration that made Yemen the poorest country in the Arab world. Few families controlled the wealth. People have struggled to survive the corruptions just to live to the next day. A person who is responsible for five children with an average of 2 USD a day has to find another way to survive. This is the reality that motivated the Yemenis to revolt.

However, the revolution made the economic situation even worst. The country was divided between two strong parties in a situation where none of them could force the other to quit the game. Instead, they chose to keep making the citizens suffer. Life in Yemen was always different and difficult than in any other countries in the region. On public buses, one could see a political discussion on the latest events with all the different viewpoints, and people would simply curse the president publicly with no fears of being arrested. Normally political discussions are held during the afternoons Qat chewing sessions, which is a social custom. However, this political discussion that raised the awareness of the corruption in the country made some people think Yemen is a democratic country especially when compared to the Gulf states and other Arab countries. However, this limited freedom of expression never resulted in change or reforms. So what's the point of having the people criticize and discuss if nothing changes eventually?

During the 2011 revolution in Yemen against President Ali Abdullah Saleh, Saleh repeated that he brought about democracy in Yemen and that he allowed the people to criticize him like no other in the region did. Simply put, he messed it up because real democracy is when criticism brings change. The reality was different, in order to get their democracy the people of Yemen needed to protest and face different kinds of violence and depravation in the streets for more than a year. Over 2000 civilian were killed for the president to understand that the game is over and the people need to enjoy their rights. And still they are struggling in the mess that he left. The question now is did they get what they sacrificed for? I would say no and we have not even gotten close to it. The lesson learnt here is that revolutions are not as glorious as they sound in history books.

I once reported on Salim Al-Harazi, a 10 year old who happened to be at the protest site praying the Friday paryer with the crowed on March 18, 2011, which was the Friday of Dignity when snipers first started killing the protesters. They killed 52 people and wounded more than 200. Salim, the little boy who is the only son among eight daughters for a very poor family, was in Change Square "the protest sight" because he enjoyed the gathering, and he like feeling a part of something bigger that can't be easily described.

When the shooting started, Salim ran towards the place the shooting comes from, like most of the others ran when the wounded called for help. Then in one second he was targeted by a sniper who heartlessly decided to shoot a ten years old boy for being there in the right place at the wrong time.

Nothing more can make you regret a revolution than a child lying down in the hospital, hardly breathing when both of his eyes are sown shut due to the shot in one eye and he tries to cry from the pain. But the tear can't find a way out in his sowed eyes. "My eyes are burning, Mother, when are you buying me a computer?" he asked while trying to get his tears out. I watched his tears trying to find their way out. I was taught as a journalist to stay neutral when covering a story, but I the human being inside of me refused at that moment to put my feeling aside and instead let the feelings out. I cried instead of Salim. And I yet didn't understand how someone could snipe someone else let alone sniping a ten is a ten years old kid.

This story might explain why I feel that our martyrs who died for justice wasted their lives for nothing. As a human rights reporter I saw more sadness behind the scenes of the Arab Spring than happiness, but in those happy times I felt like this worth all the pain. If I could go back, I would take the same path I did. I would go through it all again for these few moments. I have always had this question in my head: would people protest again if they knew the cost of the revolution? I wrote once an article that talks about the human cost of the Yemeni revolution it is a real pain when one could simply count how many lives were lost, when a human being turns into a number. I have always believed in this Quran Verse "Whoever slays a soul, unless it be for manslaughter or for mischief in the land, it is as though he slew all men, and whoever keeps it alive, it is as though he kept alive all men" meaning that a human soul can never equate the killing one life to the killing of all the lives on the earth. I strongly believe in this.

Once people start to talk numbers we have to watch out for our values. I remember a good friend of mine asking me what would make the international community pay attention to the Yemen revolution if the mainstream media keeps neglecting us. I could not think of anything that would make an editor of any newspaper call me to write a story but larger number of martyrs.

There is so much to be told if the international media decides it's worth the coverage. They should change their lenses that they see Yemen through. I have always said you have to come by yourself to understand Yemen; there is no fair description of its uniqueness. It's always featured badly as being most armed tribal society when it could also be seen as an advantage.

In Yemen youngsters who learn at early ages to hold the responsibility of the family, one would find family. Although it's an armed society where the public has at least 60 million pieces of weaponry, I would call Yemen a peaceful country because the public learns how not to use their weapons. The crime rate is no higher than any civilized country where citizens are not armed. The revolution They die for their beliefs. A video on Al-Jazeera showed how protesters in Yemen didn't move and kept doing their prayers while they were shot at by snipers.

The revolution was a call for justice but it ended the most unjust way.

Following March 18, after an attack that left 52 protesters killed by the sniper and change the game's rule, the news of officials resigned from the government and the military continued for days. Protesters forgot the painful events feeling victory that the regime is collapsing or that was what they thought.

People started dancing and chanting "Haya bohm, haya bohm" meaning welcome, welcome by the entrance of the change square. I did not feel good about it. I thought that those who did not join in the beginning they did not care about what had happened. Nothing was hidden and everyone knew the life conditions that led the protesters to put their lives at risk, but they simply did not care. But only when they thought Ali Abdullah Saleh's position was getting weak did they think it safe for them to join the revolution.

On March 21, the biggest news erupted—Major General Ali Mohsen defection of Saleh's military. Should he even be welcomed in the square my friends and I wondered since his hands are also dirty with Yemenis blood and since he is as bad as Saleh himself? I recalled then how close he was to Saleh, as a friend and partner. Somehow, at least since Saleh came to power in 1978 until the three weeks before his defection in Feb 24, I was called by the presidency secretary to negotiate the youth position with Saleh. I went, but not for the negotiation as much as to make a statement and tell him to step down. At the closed meeting I had with Saleh in his Palace, General Mohsen was setting right next to him like a brother and protector. This was only three weeks before his defection.

The Guardian:

The revolution was messed up once the defection of the military started. We accepted the regime's heads among us, those who joined to protect their interests played it well and controlled the scene. With the help of the international intervention that in Yemen played a different role than it does in other countries in the region. That role was a very strong one. It tried to kill the revolution as a revolution and made it seem like a political crises. It made us feel, as Yemenis, that as the people of the country we are politically immature need to decide on our behalf and play the role of guardian. As Yemenis, we have always faced this strange situation when someone else plays the guardian role for us. The political leadership of the country has always treated us as political juveniles. There is the lack of representation, and huge corruption and nepotism. These are not only practiced by the regime but also by the oppositional political parties as well, who practiced the same dictatorships within their parties and authorities.

People were excluded from their political right to decide for themselves; Moreover, they were dragged into different wars that many lost their lives for, but many did not know what they were fighting against. A political agreement to transfer power peacefully was proposed by the Gulf Countries. They urged all the political players to get involved and sign the agreements that will make Saleh leave his post power. But in return the agreement took a lot of rights of Yemenis under the name of saving Yemen from a highly possible civil war. The agreement started on two phases. The transitional period: the first starts the day the agreement is signed by Saleh and the opposition political parties coalition, neglecting all the others in the squares or the main actors who caused the revolution. The second phase: it starts with forced early election with only one candidate which is the vice president of Saleh for 18 years. There was nothing satisfying about this agreement. And both parties who signed were forced to by the international community and the donors. After electing the one candidate a National interim government was appointed half from what was the ruling party and half from what was the political opposition. only three women were appointed ministers, but they are not an effective mnistries. If the revolutionaries who were snapped in their back by their political agreement were stepped on once, the women revolutionaries were stepped on twice. As I mentioned, women from the first days were not allowed to participate in the day of rage. While women has a major role to start in the protest in Yemen, now those roles were also neglected. In the revolution, a woman needed to have doubled what a man has. The Yemeni women needed to revolt twice, once against the family and society rules that looks down at her in some points, and the second was revolting as an equal citizen demanding the topple of the regime to rebuild the country.

There was a small gain for women from the revolution as it made the society accept the fact the women have voices to be heard, In April 2011, Saleh made a comment during the Friday prayer to his followers. He said that what the revolutionary women do in Change Square is Islamicly forbidden, meaning that women are not allowed to protest with men. This comment made a defection among the revolutionaries; the Islamist party members followed Saleh's opinion although he was their enemy. The next morning female activists went marching against what Saleh said with their male colleagues, but the painful fact was that they were physically attacked not by Saleh thugs, but by the defected army that is supposed to support the revolution and attacked by the Islams. They were punished for enacting their rights by those with who shared the hope of building a civil state. The political agreement for power transition mentioned that there have to be women representation on the different committees that emerges as a result of the agreement. But it did not state the percentage of this representation, so it's always the minimum. Post Arab revolution, women rights became a controversial subject. Watching the fear of losing women rights that were already given to them after long struggle in Tunisia, Egypt or Libya shows how similar the result of these revolutions are when it comes to Women rights.

In Yemen, the revolutionaries sought more freedoms and rights. However, this was not the case for women. To intimidate a woman to practice her rights is much easier than men. The regime did not need to kill or detain them. Instead they can just ruin a female activist's reputation. And the impact that this could make is enough to horrify any woman away from demanding her rights or raising her voice. Badria al-Ghail is a female activist in the revolution. This was a controversial case as well. She was kidnapped by the political security from change square. Later on the authorities denied the kidnapping and made up a story that she was caught at her boyfriend's house and she was found guilty by the court. The social injustices was shown clearly. Families put more restrictions on their girls. Some were prevented from going to schools, some from protesting, and mostly girls were sent back to their villages where they stay at home. When the alarm of war was raised, the girls were told to dress decently in black in case they got injured. This they insure that their bodies were covered. Most of the interviewed parents would prefer their daughters to die than to be exposed to rape. On a political level, women have to raise their voices higher to be heard. They could be easily neglected and used as a tool of propaganda for any political party to gain more votes. Women activists called for a Women's National conference to unify women's voices and make sure they are involved in the National Dialogue that will draw the lines to the future of Yemen. They recall the historical role of Women in ancient Yemen when it was led by a woman, Queen Sheba. During the revolution many women had brave, leading roles. In October of 2011, the Nobel Peace Prize went to a Yemeni human rights female activist, Tawakkol Karman, who was one of the first to call for the revolution in Yemen. I myself was awarded the Global Trailblazer award by Vital Voices in June 2012 for my news coverage during the revolution and for my role in social media activism. I remembered that when the Tunisian President stepped down I was one of the few people in Yemen who posted on Facebook "the people want to topple the regime." Back then, I worried my people, and they literally told me to stop being crazy and to remember that I am "a girl." A month later, most of my friends posted the same states. I guess revolutions need "crazy girls" to start and a "crazy politicians" to get messed up.

Mirelle Karam Halim

EGYPT

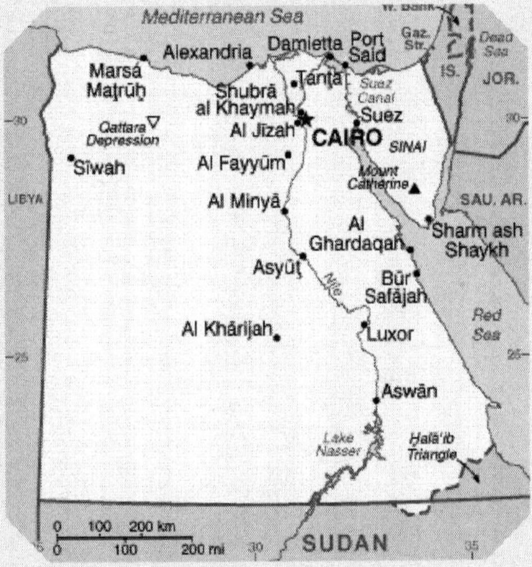

BEHIND THE SCENES...

Life...a four letter word, yet it varies so vastly from one to another, one can read it with joy, another with pain, one with mixed emotions but in the end we all live it and we all, at some point or another, feel sorrow, happiness or even emptiness.

Being a girl in Egypt certainly is an experience worth sharing, it's just like a roller coaster ride, sometimes it takes you up real high and at other times stoops you up real low. It twists and turns and flips you over from one side to the other and just when you think you're at the top and you can almost feel that fresh air gently touching your cheeks, allowing you to finally breathe in deeply, in a blink of an eye it takes you down again. This is the best way to describe my ride so far.

I may be young but certainly my roller coaster has taken me so far on a wonder ride, and I would like to take you for a quick tour with me just to give you a taste of how it's like for a girl to grow up in busy, insane, lovely, lonely, ever intoxicating Cairo.

School

I guess I'll have to start from the very beginning, School. I come from an educated family, my grandmother, Mother and father always taught me the importance and value of education; they are all reading buffs and there's nothing they value more than a good book, they have always encouraged me to do the same and have always told me that a single book can actually turn one's life around. I owe to them everything I am and I hope they know how thankful I am.
High school years, those are the greatest times in anyone's life, right? One is so young, free and without a care in the world, those are the years that ultimately sculpt your personality and shape and define the person you will become. But in fact high school in the current education system of my country is quite different: they enforce a great deal of pressure, stress and drama on the student's life and his parents that has always puzzled me. You see, we have in high school the curse of the "Private lessons", those are basically lessons that you have to take for the same subjects that are given at school but are repeated in the form of a private lesson after school in private education centers or at homes! So this means that the student takes the same subjects twice, once at his/her school and then after the school in the form of this private lessons! And let me tell you something too, these lessons don't come cheaply, they cost a FORTUNE and they put such strain financially on the poor families of the students that really makes me feel sorry for them and for what they go through.

Of course this financial strain that is imposed on the family has its effects on the student as well, at home parents chant the "NO song" to their children, so no Television, no talking too much on the phone, no going out, no no no 100 NOs, I even know families that removed the television from their daughter's room for the 2 years of her high school. This puts a tremendous pressure on the students to spend all of their time studying in order to finally justify all the stress and the sacrifices that the whole family endures, besides the fact that those private lessons don't allow the student to have the time for any form of social activities or even give them the chance to explore their talents and what they really like to do. Now imagine the student who is always under pressure, always studying, not having any time for any form of social activities or hobbies and feeling guilty for the financial burden that is enforced on his/her family and for the sacrifices they make. Is this a healthy environment for someone to grow up into? I for one hated my high school years and all the drama that came along with it and this really shouldn't be the case as I should be smiling when remembering my high school years ☺.

I will tell you the reason for all the drama I just described, and why I call these 2 years "the compass of destiny". You see the score that you get after graduation from high school is perhaps one of the most important set of numbers in your life. It literally can set your whole life in one direction or the other. If you manage to get a high score, then you'll get the chance to go into the "Top schools" that are considered to be every parent's dream, those are of course medical or engineering schools. If not, you'll wind up somewhere else then. There are cases where the student wants to go to any other school or to study anything else, but because of the high score that he/she got, their parents would force them to enter those "Top schools" against their will, so you don't really get to choose here!

I consider this to be one of the major problems in our education; children must be taught and raised on how to choose, what are the attributes to base their decision on in order for it to be right? See this is a problem, we receive information but we don't think, we study but we don't understand, we don't make our own decisions, our own choices. People cannot be forced into something and then end up losing precious years of their life when they already know what they want, why don't you get to choose what you want to study even if you didn't get the score that gets you there? Why do we always receive instead of think, why do we contribute to the loss of all the potential for these young minds, why do parents think for their kids and draw and map their future for them instead of teaching them how to draw it out and helping, supporting and enabling them with the tools to do it for themselves. If a parent's dream was always to become a doctor, then this is his dream and not their son's, No one should waste their lives to fulfill and live someone else's life, it just doesn't work.

After successfully surviving those horrific years of high school, you'll finally get the chance to go on to college (whatever it is) and start this fresh and exciting part of your life. You get the chance to live your life and you are ready for all those exciting adventures that you've read and heard about and you're not in school any more so you're grown up and ready to enjoy more freedom. Well not yet!

College

Life inside college is quite interesting; you see, I discovered that there were 2 different types of girls, ones who talk and befriend boys and others who don't and choose to stay alone to themselves and their fellow female only friends. Sometimes you would enter the lecture classroom finding the boys on the left side and the girls on the right side in complete separation, and this makes you really wonder: Which year is this again?!! Other times you'd find that girls who consider talking to boys would make people think she is impolite and some are even afraid to be seen just talking to boys in public places. Yes, unfortunately, you've read this correctly.

I come from a very reasonable background that is neither extremely open-minded nor too conservative and I am very thankful for that fact, as it allowed me to be able to understand and absorb the different point of views and perceptions on the same subject. But when it comes to this dualism and complications in the relationships with the opposite sex I am always puzzled and astonished by this matter. Being raised differently, I have always wondered how this avoidance for the normal relationships or interactions with the opposite sex work out and how this moral separation will impact the lives of the those youth after graduation and throughout their lives, I mean the society isn't separated so how do these moral stigmas thrive and work? I even at some point started questioning my own ideas and beliefs, whether I was the person who is wrong, and I questioned whether I should do the same to be considered a "good girl"? But now, being older, I understand that we behave in this way in our societies basically because we are afraid of each other and afraid of people's opinions and what they might think about us. So as long as no one can see a girl taking to a guy, smoking a cigarette, holding hands, then she must be fine, a good girl! Yes this is unfortunately the type of hypocritical society that we're living in: a girl can smoke as much cigarettes as she wants, but in the ladies room; she can talk to guys as much as she likes, but on the phone or away from people's eyes; you can wear what you want but only if you're travelling abroad where no one from home can see you! And girls typically want to maintain this "good girl" image because they are afraid of one another and of the society, doesn't matter what you do in the dark as long it stays in the dark, I have always wondered about that concept but came to the fact that it is the reality in the Arab world in general because I hear similar stories all over the region!

You see In Arab societies social stigmas and standards matter a lot, and the perception of a certain act, is even more important than the act itself or its meaning, and the more you will come to terms with that fact and digest it well the more you will be able to understand how Arab communities work.

Now the main reason for all of the above for girls is a simple word, Marriage!!!

Marriage

Oh my god I need a lot of time to talk about that in my country… oh boy, where do I start?

Of course being an Arab girl I cannot simply skip something crucial (or perceived as crucial) as marriage!

Starting from college, parents talk with Egyptian girls about marriage (and sometimes, they start even earlier!), but I will talk about the average, most common case. The mother comes and keeps asking the same question over and over again and it's like all the Arab moms have that same track playing:- "Is there someone?"

I have to be fair my mom didn't ask me that question until I finished school and found a job, but the minute I found the job she started: -

"Is there someone?"
"Umm, no, mom, there isn't anyone?"

At first she would settle with this answer, but then after few months she would go:
"So, Is there anyone?"
"No mom, again there isn't"
"Why"
"Why what mom, what do you want me to do?"
"How come there isn't, you know a lot of people, look at your friends they are all getting married"

See; read again what she said; "look at your friends"

This is it, everyone is keeping an eye on the other and wanting to go through the same way as they are going, this is the rule for a lot of things, just going with the flow, close your eyes and go along with everyone else without any questions, is that right or wrong? Do I want that or not? If I did that am I going to be happy? Do I have to say yes blindly?

Why are we so afraid of each other, why do we care that much about what other people think? Why do we all have to do the same? Aren't we different people having different needs and desires in life?

Why are Arab girls so oppressed in a cage of old ideas constructed by their parents and locked and sealed by society, and why do women apply the same cage to their daughters?

Why do we shortcut women in the word "Marriage"? If a woman accomplished a great deal of success in her life on so many levels but she wasn't married, it's like she has done nothing throughout her life! And this is truly a shame.
Women's rights have always been a sensitive topic and it is becoming worse!!

If we want to dig into the reasons for the revolution, if we want to know why we stood silent to Mubarak's regime for 30 years, we will discover that it is all related, it's because we go blindly with the flow!! Yes it is all connected to each other; we have to understand the mentality of the society to see why it took us so long to finally make a revolution and why we finally did one in the first place.

Revolution

25th of January took us all by surprise, I saw the page on Facebook and I remember finding some hope in it—even my friends were laughing at me, but in the end I was, along with many others, a person who never believed it would turn out to be serious. We all thought that it was just going to be one day and that is it, then all will be over and evaporate in a matter of hours; but we all also thought "what if?" Two powerful words that can make miracles and open up endless possibilities, and they did.

The revolution gave us hope, that the word "Change" still exists in our dictionary, that we don't have to stand silent and go with the flow again, we did a great revolution, one that the whole world was talking about, but is it enough? Have we reached our goal? Is this what we really wanted in the first place? In my opinion we are not even close to our goals. We didn't accomplish anything except overthrowing Mubarak, knowing that nothing lasts forever, that our will can really make a difference; I myself felt extremely proud after the revolution, I felt like I can really do something: I felt empowered.

I can honestly see with my own eyes the difference right now between the spirit that we had during the revolution and the chaos that is happening right now: I can see what's going on. When I went to Tahrir Square, it was such a beautiful scene, with wonderful harmony among people. There were college students, employees from multinational corporates, simple workers and craftsmen, , Muslims, Christians, liberals and conservatives, all sitting together in the heart of Cairo and helping each other. There was one group forming a circle together and reciting poetry, another group was gathered around singing, and some were writing the word "erhal" which means "leave" on the walls of the buildings. Such different and diverse streams of people representing every population of people existing in Egypt, yet still coexisting in perfect harmony that makes you really proud for being an Egyptian. Nobody harassed anyone. Women were very safe and were never harassed!—and this is the Tahrir Square we're talking about here, for that amount of population to be in such a small space, usually people would be squeezing each other. I witnessed something very surprising. Whenever a guy touched you by mistake or slammed into you, he said "Sorry, I didn't mean it." People were protecting each other.

What we saw there, that's our future, that's what we looked up for in the upcoming days. It was like a vision. Look - These are the Egyptians. Look what they can do. We all believed in it and it was just beautiful. I know maybe you may have heard that a lot of times but it was like a scene from a movie or something, an imaginary scene. Nobody could ever believe how organized it was, how respectful it was, and how decent and civilized the people were, it was just beautiful.

Now where did it all go?

The chaos that we are seeing now is nothing compared to what we've seen before the revolution. But still it makes me question, what happened, what went wrong and why? My interpretation of this situation is that in the beginning, we were all united for one goal, to overthrow a tyrant. Everybody was shouting from their hearts for that reason and we all felt we were united for the same cause, we come from the same place, we are Egyptians, and we are one. There were no barriers between us, no gender differences, no religious differences and no social classes that divide us, nothing. That's why everybody was just so focused on that goal, believing in it and being able to see the bigger picture. What happened after revolution is that people now have different goals, now people are divided, and everyone is seeking their own interests, so we became so focused and consumed in the details and personal trivial gains that we've lost sight of the bigger picture.

Egyptians are very smart – we really are smart people. I totally believe that, you see everyone talking politics now, everyone is debating, some people even got into fights because of political debates, despite this, my personal feeling is that it is a very healthy sign that folks are starting to talk about politics after decades of silence and oppression. The Debate itself and the uncertainty of the result of elections, this is healthy. This is what we really want; this is what we've been looking for. It's perfectly healthy to debate who will win the next elections. The debate and the uncertainty of the results is, in my opinion, one of the gains.

Misuse of religion

Pharaoh Egyptians were the first civilization to ever believe in the existence of a god, and Egyptians in general are a very religious, simple and god fearing people, and unfortunately certain people misuse this faith and the huge amount of trust that any simple Egyptian places in the religious representatives. Certain people sometimes misuse religion in influencing others, and the way people are manipulated by the name of religion, is for me, a true crime that should have a law placed against it. The complete separation of religion from the state should be settled. It's a crucial pillar for a healthy society, and if we cannot reach that complete and total separation, then at least we should not allow or tolerate the use of religion in manipulating people. What's more obnoxious even is that some people use their social power and the fact that simple people trust, follow and believe them, to start taking advantage of this trust and to start questioning the faith or the degree of commitment to religion for others. This is just ugly and such acts are the ones responsible for the delay and deteriorations of complete nations, this is bad when it happens in society, but when it happens in politics, it is just unfair and disastrous.

Women's rights

Unfortunately the usage of religion in politics and their combination tends to affect women as well, and its impact is even larger. I will simply state a situation that occurred during the past parliamentary elections where one of the Salafi's(the most conservative Muslims) party actually placed the picture of a rose instead of the face women who were running for parliament—because a picture of a woman was deemed as not proper to be shown to the public! And, as a result of these actions, women held 2% of parliamentary seats in comparison to 12% in the previous elections, and not one woman ended up taking part in participating in the committee that wrote the constitutional amendments!

So yes, it affects women negatively, but eventually we're all in the same boat here, and the misuse of religion and the manipulation of people affect us all. It affects minorities; Christians and also affects the moderate majority as well. That's a strong battle, a powerful battle, but we should continue because simply there's no other option for our country but to win.

It is important to remember, that the level of women in Tahrir Square was almost equal to men, and I've witnessed it myself, they were almost equal in numbers to men, and actually statistics have shown that the level of participation by women in the revolution was 47 to 50%. Girls and women do everything, share everything whether it's good or bad, they are simply the half of our society, but they are not represented in the crucial political decision-making process. That's the gap here. They are almost in every other job. They are just not in the decision-making jobs.

Women are expanding the role themselves. They are doing that right now, women are finally doing something. **They are willing to enact a change of**

course; this is just a little bit harder to do because of the stereotypes and cultural norms. But I have come to realize, for example, that closed communities does not necessarily mean that women cannot go to work, cannot travel, cannot stay late at night or spend the night outside even. It doesn't mean that at all, which was a revelation to me, because I work in development projects and a lot of my work is with girls in closed communities who volunteer and who want to do something for their communities and I think that's a great progress itself. That's against the stereotypical idea of women staying at home and it's very, very important to see these girls doing something constructive for their communities.

That's what we have to fight for, women to go get their rights and to participate in the development and prosper of their communities, that's what we have to gain, definitely. The will is there, and where there is a will there is always a way, but we have to fight to gain that right, especially with the rise of conservative Islamists taking place, and the existence of some attempts to diminish those rights and their importance, by really reconstructing those stereotypical ideas and emphasizing their alleged importance. That's why the battle is getting harder and harder, and I firmly believe that those rights will be obtained with the men in the communities believing and adopting them as well.

What we really need now is a self-revolution, revolution on our own outdated ideas that we jail ourselves in: revolution on our perception of women, relationships and even life itself, a revolution on our community and what we consider to be important. We need a revolution on how we treat each other and on every single act we do: a revolution against those who try to forbid the god given rights of freedom from anyone.

My thoughts may have been distracting in some instances here, but I think they reflect the state of which my beloved country is going through. I may have been harsh, judgmental or even angry sometimes, but I believe in exposing everything and showing the naked and sometimes ugly truth, so that we can start working on them. It is only from my deep love for this country that I am still trying to figure out the secret to its spell that everyone falls under, is it the heart melting smile of the guy I meet every day trying to sell me flowers or the kindness and the innocence of the old lady selling veggies around the corner! .. I don't know but I do know that Egyptians are among the best in the world and we certainly deserve so much better, better education, better economy and better politicians who fight for their rights for a change.

This era is the era of revolutions, revolutions will keep going until all rights are granted everywhere in the world, not just in the Arab world. There is this awakening that happened to people around the world no matter what their causes might be, but the silent days are gone. I am one of the people who is trying to make a self-revolution after realizing that there is more to life. I keep discovering that each day, there are more choices, more options, more everything! I reached this conclusion myself after hearing it a lot before, yet I never fully grasped it's true meaning or believed in it, but the fact is yes it is true, we should question everything and not take anything for granted. There are many locked doors in our mind that I believe, when learning new things, knowing more and experiencing more in life will eventually grant us the keys to those locks, one after the other. After having my own revolution, this was one of the primary rules that I have placed for myself: I will always keep exploring, discovering and unlocking doors. Remember, there is more out there than our little world in which we set its boundaries. We should never cease to understand more about ourselves, to be challenged and amazed, and we should always reach out to our true purpose and meaning in this life.

Raghda Abushahla

PALESTINE

Due to the Israel/Palestine conflict, the borders are continually reconfigured and a map could not be provided at this time.

LIFE IN GAZA:
A PALESTINIAN WOMAN'S PERSPECTIVE

Preface

I would like to write about Palestinian people and more precisely about Palestinian women. I want to write also about my personal experience as a Palestinian woman from Gaza living under difficult conditions. I want to share with people the things that lead me in life.

I don't want to be a wave of change, I don't want to be the leader of a revolution and I don't want to be the one implementing political reforms. It is simple; I don't want to be the lead player in the scene because I would rather be the essential player of the same scene. The absence of this essential player will destroy the whole scene. I don't want to be a wave of change in my country because I prefer to be the undercurrent that creates and leads this wave. This is my character as well as most of Palestinian women. We are the ones who keep the society together; we are the strength and the rock that carries the heavy burdens of life. Yet we still know exactly how to love, care, survive and promise hope and happiness to our men and our children.

We Palestinian women are strong; we have to be strong because it is our destiny. It is the destiny of the women, particularly from Gaza, who are meant to be the source of strength for Palestine.

Life in Palestine

Her name is Khadeeja Tawsis / Abu-Shahla, the pride of my family, the strong old lady whose life follows the history of Palestine "Philistine in history books." She is old, yet still strong. Years had taken from her health but gave her wisdom, strength and tenderness at the same time. She was born decades before the 1948 War. She was even married and gave birth to her first three sons before that year.

Life was not easy with her; I usually like to say that she is "Life"... Her life is the example of how strong determined achievers Palestinian women are, and happy as well, regardless of all the sorrows and hardships life had put on their way. They are happy because they achieve their goals, and my grandmother's goal was opening her children to knowledge and providing them with solid education. She believed that education is the way to ensure a better future for them, their offspring, and generations to come. She was right with her belief because my grandparents were not wealthy, and they had no inheritance to leave for their children except providing them with the means to help themselves. That's why my grandmother insisted on educating all her nine children. This old beloved lady who was born and grew up in Akko in the historic Palestine, then married and lived in Gaza with no possibility to go visit her childhood home even once before she kisses life goodbye.

Many wars stormed Palestine over history including the 1948 War (Al-Nakba), the 1967 Six Days War, and the Operation Cast Lead on Gaza . . . the Intifada, the recurring Israeli invasions, the internal clashes, and on and on. During wars, unfortunately, civilians suffer the most. My grandmother, my mother, my sisters, women in my family and in my society and I play the biggest role in reducing this suffering for the sake of our families, children and beloved ones. We are the strength that our community thread relies on.

I was born in 1979 in Tripoli, the capital of Libya, to Palestinian parents. My story doesn't start at this date; my story goes far beyond in time. It started centuries ago when my city Gaza was born. However, I will start my personal story as a Palestinian woman from Gaza in the year 1967 and the 6 Days War.

I was born in Libya to a Palestinian family which doesn't hold any kind of citizenship; my situation did not change until the year 1995. Although in some states a person will get the nationality of the country he/she is born in, it is not usually applicable in the Arab world.

As far as my family tree goes back through history, many generations ago, I am Palestinian. My paternal and maternal ancestry is from Gaza, West Bank and Akko. My father and his forefathers are from Gaza; specifically from Al-Daraj neighborhood; one of the deep-rooted neighborhoods in Gaza city.
For those who do not know about Gaza city, it is a Palestinian city located in

the Gaza Strip inhabited since at least the 15th-century BCE. Archaeological researches have proven that Gaza is one of the oldest cities in the world. From its beginnings, Gaza was doomed to be the land bridge and meeting place and battlefield of great empires – Egypt, Assyria, Babylonia, the Hellenistic kingdoms, Rome and the Ottomans. Their peoples and armies moved up and down the way of the Sea, one of the oldest roads in the world, which spanned the country from North to South. It is situated in a strategic location as a trade path between the continents of Asia and Africa, and between the desert and the Mediterranean. Although all the historical dynasties of the Middle East fought to possess Gaza, the citizens of Gaza have shown their determination and vitality over centuries. One can enjoy the beautiful seashore and wonderful hospitality of the Gazans.

Described by the media as a war torn region, one would be surprised to find the city of Gaza rather a vibrant one. There are hospitals, schools, universities, shops, cars, hotels, fireworks at night and many people enjoying the beach. With a population of approximately 1.5 million in a small area of approximately 365 km2, there are people everywhere in Gaza. The city is vivid even with the marks of bullets and shrapnel on many buildings and the remnants of houses destroyed by the F16 rockets and tank shells. Even with the boys working hard after school in young ages to support their families, I am proud of Palestine and Gaza.

Commonwealth Cemetery

During World War I Gaza fell to British forces becoming a part of the British Mandate of Palestine. This picture is for the Commonwealth Gaza War Cemeteries, and we Gazans usually call them the British War Cemeteries, they are the cemeteries where you can find the graves of the fallen Allied soldiers in the Great War. The cemetery in the picture is located at the Tuffah neighborhood. This might be the only place in Gaza city in which you can see green areas paying respect to these soldiers. Gaza Muslim families are looking after these cemeteries and taking care of them. People in Gaza respect the idea that theses soldiers are unified together after their death regardless of their nationality, color, religion or ethnicity. You will find graves of Muslims, Christians and Jews from various nationalities. You will also find engraved on those gravestones the Christian Cross, the Jewish Star and Muslim verses of Quran. All those graves in this place of tranquility and peace; the two things that we are yearning for in the Gaza Strip, It fascinates us how beautiful it would be if this unity were applied to the living not only for the dead.

A Brief History of the Gaza Strip

As a result of the 1948 War (Al-Nakba), Egypt administered the Gaza Strip territory. Then Gaza was occupied by Israel in the Six-Day War in 1967, and remained under Israeli administration for almost three decades. Then in 1993, the city was transferred to the Palestinian National Authority following the Oslo Accords signed between Israel and the Palestinian Liberation Organization. According to the Oslo accords, the Palestinian Authority was set up as temporary body to govern part of the Palestinian areas, with Israel maintaining control of Gaza Strip's airspace, territorial waters, all its land borders, and the Israeli settlements that were eating most of the Gaza Strip land, until a final agreement could be reached between the two sides, and which is not reached until this moment. In 2005 Israel unilaterally disengaged from the Gaza Strip.

This was not the last challenge for Gaza; this was yet another challenge. Since the Israeli withdrawal, the Hamas political party and its rival Fatah were engaged in a struggle for power. On January 25, 2006, Hamas won the elections for the Palestinian Legislative Council, the legislature of the Palestinian National Authority. Then shortly after; Hamas overthrew Fatah forces in the Gaza Strip in 2007 and Israel imposed a blockade over the Gaza Strip. Until this date Hamas has de facto control over the Gaza and Israel is still imposing the blockade over the Strip.

The Israeli blockade of the Gaza Strip is causing the humanitarian situation in Gaza to reach its worst level since Israel occupied the entire Gaza Strip in the 1967 War according to the statement by a coalition of human rights groups in March 2008. The Israeli air strikes targeting militants in the densely populated and crowded areas have many times killed innocent bystanders and civilians as well. In 2008, Israel carried out war against Gaza known as Operation Cast Lead. Israel stated that they launched this war in response to homemade rockets and mortar attacks from the Gaza Strip into Israel since 2005, while the Palestinian militants stated that they were responding to Israel's repetitive military incursions and blockade of the Gaza Strip.

The Humanitarian Crisis in Gaza

Imagine the damage this war can do in such a densely populated area; imagine the rockets fired by the F16 war planes over the heads of civilians. Gaza's population is composed of a Muslim majority and Christian Minority; in addition to a massive flow of Palestinian refugees, Christians and Muslims that multiplied the Gaza's population after the 1948 (Al-Nakba). The city's population has continued to increase since that time and the city has seen a rise in poverty, unemployment, and poor living conditions that are widespread. Gaza has serious deficiencies in housing and infrastructure, and a poor sewage system has contributed to serious problems of hygiene and public health. The Gaza population is suffering from approaching sanitary disasters because of the water and sewage problems. The sewage in the cesspools leaks back into the coastal aquifer, which is the only source of freshwater for Gaza's 1.5 million people. The more the aquifer is being used, the more salty and contaminated it becomes. And the Gaza sewage is pumped into the sea in some areas along the shore in Gaza because of lacking the proper infrastructure to process the waste.

Gazans are marked as terrorists and imprisoned in the Gaza enclave for so many years with severe shortages of money, electricity, fuel, and other essential life commodities. Nevertheless, a small percent of the Gaza population is in possession of weapons or rockets. The vast majority of the population were middle class people who suffered years of hardships and now live in poor conditions and aspire to survive.

However, the symbol of Gaza is the phoenix, the legendary bird. The phoenix is a beautiful, mythical bird, and its legend exists in many cultures. Basically, it is large bird that lives for many years until his life approaches its end at which time the Phoenix builds a nest and lights the nest and itself on fire. Out of the ashes a new phoenix would be born. This rebirth represents Gaza; like the phoenix, the city is again and again born from its ashes to survive.

Gazans as the rest of Palestinians are proud people and very much alive. They are strong and resilient. They know how to enjoy their life and they know how to seek a better future. They respect the past, live the day and view the future with hope. These characteristics are very strong in the Palestinian blood and are difficult to change, regardless of many difficult situations they faced throughout history, and particularly during the last 64 years of occupation. What makes me proud the most is that Gaza in Arabic language is feminine. My Gaza is a female like me. Our symbol the phoenix (Al-Anquaa) is a female in Arabic language, too.

As with any conflict, whether racial, religious or political, those hit hardest are the people; those normal civilians who have never actually participated in it or even supported it. Yet luckily Gazans remain to be friendly hardworking people with never ending optimism.

It is the people of Gaza that have the greatest impression on anyone; they are such a welcoming and hospitable society. It is their challenging situation that makes them even more positive, and despite the difficulties they are faced with, together they strive without rest to develop Gaza and Palestine.

As I mentioned earlier, my story goes back to the year 1967, when my father was pursuing his university education in Egypt. He is originally from Gaza – Palestine. His family up to many generations back in history is from Gaza. My family had very deep roots in Gaza.

My father was born and lived there until he was about eighteen years old. Then he travelled to Egypt before the 1967 War to attend to university there because in my family, thanks to our strong and wise female ancestors, higher education is very important and crucial in one's life. My grandparents in Gaza had nine children; seven boys and two girls. All of them completed their university education even though there were no universities in Gaza at the time, even though my grandfather was not a rich man. My grandmother made it her mandate to make it possible for her children to receive proper education; she made it her role in life, as every other Palestinian woman in my country, to make available the best options in life for her children.

My simple old grandparents were saving as much as they can from their humble income, earned by my grandfather to send the three older sons to receive their education in Cairo, including my father, and then followed by my oldest aunt. When it was time for the second generation of brothers and sisters to go to university, the older brothers had already graduated, with jobs and sending money to the younger brothers and sister to pay for their university education. One can say that my grandmother and my grandfather made sure that everyone of their offspring supported the other to achieve their degrees. It is the same issue with my generation now; we the daughters and sons of the nine brothers and sisters are supporting our younger siblings to pursue and complete their university education because this is one of the mandates of our mothers, grandmothers and female ancestors.

Back to my father, and how he ended up being a Palestinian without citizenship. He was born three years before the year, 1948. A Palestinian who lived in Gaza until it was time to go pursue his university education. When the Six Days War erupted, and Israel invaded Gaza he was studying in Egypt. Thus, he didn't get any ID "by Israel" as the rest of his siblings who became living under the Israeli occupation and being identified by the ID card / Hawiya given by the occupation authorities. Meanwhile, Egypt gave him some document named Watheka Masrya. This is a document that states that he is Palestinian. However, with this document my father was not allowed to live in Palestine. When he acquired his university degree, he moved to Libya to seek a job. There he found a job, settled in an apartment, and met my mother, a pretty Palestinian from the West Bank who was studying with her siblings in the Libyan universities. They fell in love, and got married. Three daughters and a son are the result of their happy marriage. We were all born in Libya, as Palestinians without citizenship or even Palestinian civic rights.

During our childhood we never lived in Palestine, we were denied the right to live in our country of origins because we do not have the hawiya. And life in Libya was not easy; it was a challenge to live under the Qaddafi's regime. Also life there was not peaceful because of the war on Libya due to the famous Lockerbie bombing and before that the 1986 United States bombing of Libya in response to the 1986 Berlin discotheque bombing. The USA bombed Libyan military facilities, and residential areas of Tripoli and Benghazi, on the year 1986.

I remember very well the first night of the bombing of Libya, and I think I will never forget it. Although in Gaza I am witnessing more horrors and more Israeli bombing, that night when I was just 7 years old my sense of security and safety was not broken, thanks to my beloved mother. Thinking of it now and remembering how I wake up at midnight confused by the very loud explosions, not even knowing what an explosion is at that age, I was scared. It was very loud bombing. My mother came to us and hugged us very calmly and said this is bombing but we should not worry, that it would go away shortly. Feeling her strength and her control I felt safe and calm. Many of our neighbors were in panic, yet she was even singing with us our innocent childhood songs. For a few days we were hiding from the bombing and with the love of my parents, their patience and strength we didn't feel panic or even fear. And having been, myself, subjected to many nights and days of Israeli bombing in the Gaza Strip, I know exactly what amount of strength is needed to hide her own fear, keep calm and controlled in front of kids at such times.

This was only the beginning of difficulties in Libya. Shortly after the US bombing, the UN imposed sanctions on Libya to force Qaddafi to hand over for trial two Libyan citizens that were suspected to be involved in the blowing up of a PanAm airliner over the town of Lockerbie in December 1988. We lived under sanctions for several years and it was tough for normal people like us who had nothing to do with politics. My parents only wanted to live, take care of their children, and raise them in a healthy atmosphere.

Regardless of all the difficult circumstances in Libya, my siblings and I were happy and satisfied with life, thanks to the efforts of my parents and their positivity. I now know exactly how difficult their life in Libya was. They were alone, struggling, while they grew up in big supportive families as it is the case in the Arab culture, and they found themselves alone in Libya and deprived of seeing their families. They missed their parents, brothers, sisters, cousins. They needed their families support but they couldn't get it from overseas; however, they never made us feel it.

One of the worst situations one can go through as a teenager without citizenship was when we were kept in the no man's land on the borders between Egypt and Libya (Salloum) and were stuck there in the desert for several days, no shelters, no commodities, no food, with all our belongings, fearing smugglers and thieves. What would have happened to us without the mercy of our Libyan bus drivers? … Sad to say that this was a horrible experience, I was around fifteen years old at that time, my younger sister and brother were six and five years old respectively. It was a trauma full of fear, humiliation and uncertainty of what would happen to us. Yet again the strength of my mother, father and older sister came out of nowhere to support us. We survived this ordeal by focusing on supporting my baby sister and brother through it.

When the Egyptian authorities refused to open the borders to let us out of this misery and after waiting for several long days, Libya finally opened its borders to allow us to return to Tripoli. Back to the city I was born in, back to my school but not back to our normal life, we spent one more year in Libya and then fortunately we were issued Palestinian IDs as part of the Oslo Accords with Israel. This was the end of our odd status of citizenship of nowhere.

When finally back to our city of our roots "Gaza" in 1996, meeting grandparents, aunts, uncles and cousins, and getting introduced to our extended family and feeling the difference and the strength of being part of our society, who speaks our language and shares the same origins, I felt stronger; much stronger with the support of my family and more responsible for the welfare of my family. We belong to this place, it is in our blood and we are responsible to support it, and support our people inside and outside Palestine. These are my people, and I am proud of them and I am one of the pillars of support for them to build a better and peaceful future. This is my role.

My aspiration for Palestine:

Palestine is living through difficult circumstances of lack of peace and stability. This instability is caused by many internal and external conflicts such as the Palestinian/Israeli conflict, which is ongoing for more than sixty years and led to the eruption of many wars such as the Israeli Operation Cast Lead on Gaza 2008-2009. Also, the conflict between the Palestinian leading political parties Fatah and Hamas which led to an armed conflict in 2007 in addition to the interests in conflict between the leading Arab and International players who are involved in the Palestinian/Israeli conflict.

These conflicts are causing lack of peace and stability and are hindering the possibilities of human development in Palestine. The long term effects of these conflicts are dangerous because they are spreading poverty, ignorance, frustration, and diseases, and causing more conflicts, aggressions and suffering of the Palestinian people.

Recently many efforts in Palestine are joined towards establishing a Palestinian sovereign state. In such circumstances, if a Palestinian state shall be declared one day, it will need a strong base of democratic society to lead the change in Palestine toward a democratic state.

Palestine could be an independent democratic and sovereign state where the citizens are respected, law is implemented and a fair and independent justice system is developed. People in Palestine are thriving for peace and stability. They are always eagerly hoping and yearning for a better future, if not for themselves, for their children and the next generations where these generations live in more peaceful political situations in which they determine their life and practice their rights and their freedom.

Emna Ben Yedder

TUNISIA

A RECIPE FOR ENGAGEMENT:
MANY INJUSTICES, A DOSE OF CRITICAL THINKING, AND ACTION

I want to write about engagement, about the happiness that procures the willingness to understand its source and about living it. Engagement for me is the consequence of a quest, an infinite quest. Engagement is to finite what philosophy is to infinite. I believe that engagement comes from the willingness to perfect a world that we painfully realize is too imperfect. It is a quest for meaning. Specifically, what I mean here is that I consider engagement as being a quest aimed at giving some meaning to a world that is sometime meaningless, hard.

First Discovery: The World is Meaningless

I realized that the world was meaningless at the age of 5, when I entered school. At 5 I realized that my mom had lied to me, that the beauty I had in my eyes was coming from her, from the beauty of her soul and of her heart. Before school my mom had already transmitted me the key of happiness – she had already taught me how to read. At school, instead of discovering a world of knowledge, my first discoveries were those of injustice, stupidity, and wickedness.

When I was a kid my family was living in a frontier neighborhood, where a residential middle-class neighborhood adjoined an area of very disadvantaged illegal housing inhabited by very poor families. At school, both populations were meeting each other.

The professor, who was as well the Director of the school, *killed* the meaning of school. *He killed the ideal of equality that it was supposed to bear*. Under its roof, the kids from the relatively wealthy families were placed at the first rank, although the kids from the poor families were seated at the back of the classroom. Only the latter were beaten for schoolroom gossip, even when they were not chatting. I felt the severity of this man, and his fake smile. This man wanted to perpetuate inequality. It's only much later that I understood why I hated this man who was without a heart and soul.

Second Discovery: Philosophy - The Quest of Meaning is a Science

At the age of 17, I discovered with philosophy that the quest of meaning was a science; it was a big slap in the face, a slap against order, against accommodation and the passive acceptance of already made thoughts. Our professor was the first in 1998, 12 years before the Arab Spring, to tell us that we were responsible for the government that we had in Tunisia. A dark and inhumane totalitarian regime; a government against human rights and the right to think for oneself. Torture and violation of rights were legions, and we were consenting. The government was to Tunisia what my professor was to poor kids – a demon of injustice. And I was this little girl who was seeing the drama but wasn't saying anything, who could only hate and suffocate, but didn't know where to seek this wholesome breath of fresh air. I had become this revolutionary of living rooms criticizing the system, but who wasn't even able to put a wrench in the gears.

The Spark of Engagement: General Insurrection and the Arab Spring

In December 2010, Mohamed Bouazizi and the insurgent people from Sidi Bouzid and Thela opened up the doors of possibility for us. They brought to a Tunisian people a reanimation, the wholesome oxygen they needed. They allowed the people to unite around one reason: to topple the dictator, a process which culminated on January 14th, 2011.

Everything finally seemed possible and the fear was gone. The mental barriers that were preventing us from acting were slowly being removed and this helped to reveal the potential of a people that came to be able to say *no*.

This spark gave wings to Tunisian people and the spring was offered. Tunisians were like migrating birds whom had come a long way and were tired but full of hope. Tunisians are now standing on green branches, still fragile, and the dryness and fear that they were feeling inside of their body and skin is no longer. These migrating birds are far from having arrived; democracy and a fair future are still to be built, and the specter of fear is still to be fought against. I became a street activist and during the past eighteen months we worked on civic education and cultural projects across Tunisia with fellows from the NGOs: we helped create. Now Tunisian NGO's landscape is very much flourishing: long live these initiatives and energy. I left my living room and now I will try to stay in the streets, to remain there in order to try to help and to transmit in the emergency of life anything that can help build a society of dignity, knowledge, and justice.

Youth and elder people after the revolution were all driven by this feeling that Tunisia could be reshaped for the best, that it could become a model of social justice, equality, dignity and freedom. The situation has changed much since then, and Tunisians, who do not fear anymore a common dictator, now fear the dictator that each one of us hosts inside.

Tunisia is now a society where two camps fear each other, without knowing each other, and where neither side is able to accept the other in its differences. There is a long way until Democracy is reached, and patience and respect are not the quickest values to learn.

Engagement, A New Bet: Not Engaging is More Risky than Engaging

Some believe that engaging is a risk, that some activists who dare to assert their opinions may jeopardize their future and even their lives and to be persecuted by dictators with no future. This risk exists, it is true, as men of little virtue, intoxicated by the power sink sometimes in excess and get overwhelmed with power they end up confusing with despotism. However, isn't the risk of killing one's thoughts, enthusiasm, dreams and children's future much bigger and much more crucial?

In The Pensées (Literally "Thoughts"), the philosopher Pascal compares the risk of one believing to the one not believing in God. Believing in God implies a commitment, the commitment to stick to a more pious and austere lifestyle than the one that would be procured by the absence of a master. Pascal still chose to believe, since he came to the conclusion that not to believe would lead to trade the entertainment of a lifetime to an infinite redemption. This calculation was indeed that of a mathematician and there is only a mathematician who can win faith by such arguments.

It was not faith that Pascal had won, he had only won a logical guilt and a binding conclusion, unconvincing. Pascal won faith much later, when illuminated by his thoughts; he was touched by grace, a grace that gave him the illumination of truth, beauty and greatness.

Thus, although rational engagement is a risk much more fruitful (it allows the authors to think freely, to fight for causes they believe just, to give a better future to their children) its source is not rational.

Rationality cannot mobilize people, and very few are the people that fainted when seeing a mathematical formula. The source of engagement is emotional. It arises when one realizes that the future is possible, that it can be big and beautiful, and that from now on we refuse the future to be otherwise, even if in the immediate circumstances no one can say rationally whether life can actually be otherwise.

Being irrational allows one to dream: it frees one people from mind made formulas, barriers, rules, unfair laws once thought immutable. But didn't the people of Mai 68 chant: "let's be realistic and demand for the impossible"? These people were asking for the impossible because, at that moment, this impossible was not considered as such. Realizing that the "possible" is not a determinant is what leads to commitment, belief, and the fight for one's dreams and ideas, and it is a beautiful feeling to experience this release.

This liberation could be for a poor oppressed man, what this dream could be for a small caged bird: upon closing its eyes it would imagine itself as a migrant bird flying over vast plains, and in a free move would break its cage and fly in the sky because this is where it should be, where its rightful place is.

Salma Nazzal

PALESTINE

Due to the Israel/Palestine conflict, the borders are continually reconfigured and a map could not be provided at this time.

CARRYING FAMILY TRADITIONS

I remember my Grandma pointing to an Iraqi old ruined tank . . .

My grandmother lives in a very clean house, simply furnished. It is a regular Palestinian house, in the heart of the city of Jenin, in one of those quiet neighborhoods where the houses are built out of the famous Palestinian strong white stone and topped with dark orange bricks. All the houses are surrounded by almond and citrus orchards. In the morning, you will hear nothing but the voices of the songbirds, the "Bulbul". In the afternoon, you hear the voices of kids playing football in the street.

We are sitting in her living room on a brown sofa, surround by pictures of the family hanging on the white walls, an old T.V laying on a wooden Komudino is nearby. In the corner, there is a plastic table that we drag to the middle of the room when having food in celebration of an occasion. I looked at my cousin and say "Mai I guess I won't apply this year. I don't feel like it's the proper time to travel this year. I'll postpone the application for next year." She looked back at me with worry in her eyes and said "No, don't postpone it. You might not have another chance next year. Go and work on it. Tonight."

We had this conversation in the living room, where the rest of the family were sitting, laughing, and chatting. It is a tradition in my family, a term which includes my own family, my two aunts families, and my uncles' families, to gather every Thursday night at Grandma house. The total number of people may reach 40 members on the feast nights, which we call the "Eid," the Muslim celebration after the end of the Ramadan fast, or during the Pilgrimage days, "Al-Haj," when Muslims go to Mekka asking for salvation. Even when the whole Muslim world doesn't gather in celebration though, she is always welcoming us to her house every weekend, offering us delicious food, tea, and Arabic coffee with cardamom that smells so good. During summer nights, we all gather at the veranda. In the winter, we will be all setting in a room surrounding the heater and steaming chestnuts.

My Grandmother and Her Sister in Jenin Girls High School

My Dad setting on an Iraqi Tank standing in an area near Jenin

Grandma is an old lady, about 85 years old. For me, she represents the history of Palestine. She witnessed all the historical struggles of Palestinians since the 1948 Israeli occupation, when the Jews who came to Palestine occupied the land, displaced and expelled its people. Since we were little kids, she reminds us about the experiences those in Jenin had in 1967 when a war was launched by the Arab countries against Israel to liberate Palestine and how the war ended up with a bitter defeat of the Arabs. I remember my Grandma pointing to an Iraqi old ruined tank that still stands on a mountain as a memorial of the courageous Iraqi soldiers.

She reminded us about the history of Jenin, one of the ancient cities that is still inhabited by people and was built by the Canaanites 2450 year BC, known historically as "Ein Janim" The City of Gardens as it is famous for Citrus orchards.

Grandma also told us about the time when Jenin was under the Jordanian administration, from 1948 to 1967, and how the city was decorated when the late king of Jordan Hussein came to visit the city. Her neighbors rushed into her house, which was located in the center of the city, to watch the event. At that time, the house was considered one of the finest and biggest houses in the city. My grandparents didn't own the house; it was rented. In comparison to other families, though, it was an indicator of having good income -- being able to rent such a house at that time when other families were very poor. Every time she tells us the story, she mentions every detail of the house, how the ceiling was decorated, and the large number of windows that had a view of the city's center, the small kitchen, the attic where my cousins and my dad used to hide their toys. Whenever Grandma would tell the story, when I was a little kid, I would imagine how big it was, how convenient it was for kids to have this attic to play and hide the toys without having mom asking us to keep it arranged.

King Hussein in a visit to Jenin Girls High School

Grandma also tells us about her neighbors at that time, the housewives, and what good relationships they had. She tells us about their monthly reception where she, with other neighboring women, and her friends used to join and host. They would get dressed up and have all kinds of food at the reception, how they had their own feminist conversations. She will say at that moment "All of us were housewives. We all had kids and houses to take care about every day, still we had the time to sit and talk. These days, look at women, they barley have time to speak. They're always busy with work. Unfortunately time is getting so limited for them." She was making an important notion: Life is too short. We should stop running during the day. We should have little time to stop for a while and reflect.

I was having these thoughts, still sitting in Grandma House, drinking a hot sweet cup of tea flavored with sage or as we call it "Maryamia," in reference to virgin Mary who lived in Palestine,[1] listening to my cousin Mai. She was continuing to tell me about the importance of joining this fellowship, how it's going to give me broader overview of the democratic transitions and a network of professionals. I replied at that moment "Well, I understand your point, but I would have to postpone the semester at the University. Would that be convenient for me?"

1 http://www.mariatrebenherbs.com/67/83-sage/itemid-0

At that moment, I remembered my father, may his soul rest in peace. I was pretty sure that he would be proud of me if I could join the program and still be committed to my studies when come back.

My dad (in the left) and my eldest uncle (in the middle) in my grandfather's farm

My father was an educated man. He was always encouraging my siblings and myself to pursue our education. He would never oppose any step we might take in regard to improving our education. For me, my dad was a perfect man, well educated, successful, calm, courageous and wise. I remember him telling me about how he grew up in a family of nine siblings. At that time they had to help their father during the summer vacation in planting the farm that is located in Qabatia, a village in the Jenin governorate where my family originally come from. Grandma has told me how, when my father was growing up, he had to help my Grandfather in farming and harvesting the crop, which was probably watermelon since it is one of the important crops of Jenin. My father told me himself how he went to Beirut when he was almost 16 years old to sell watermelon for my Grandfather. A story which was designed to tell us that their generation was responsible and serious. This was his way to encourage us to do a harder work.

I always looked at my father as the courageous man. This courage was especially evident when he was telling me for many times how he participated in Al-

Karameh battle in support to the Jordanian soldiers, a battle that took place in 1968 between the Jordanian Army with the support of the Palestinian militants against the Israeli Army, who tried to occupy the Eastern Bank of the Jordan River for strategic reasons. In that battle, they achieved a humble victory over the Israeli Army. And whenever I look at his picture on the wall in our house, I remember how much he was interested in politics, how during that period of our life as a family my father nominated himself for the Palestinian Legislative elections.

This was in the year 1996, three years after the establishment of the Palestinian National Authority in part of the West Bank and Gaza, which was a result of 1993 Oslo accords between Palestinian Liberation Organization and the Israeli government. The Oslo accords (officially called the Declaration of Principles on Interim Self-Government Arrangements) stated that temporary Palestinian self-government should be established in the West bank and Gaza with a Palestinian administrative control, in addition to an elected Palestinian Legislative Council for a transitional phase until both parties reach a permanent solution. The Israeli army was also to withdraw from parts of the West Bank and Gaza.

As my father was preparing himself for the campaign, the whole family supported - my uncles, my aunts, my mother, and all our relatives in our village. We were all busy. He was an independent nominee, which means he didn't represent any political party. He carefully drafted his slogan, as all nominees did, and he ended up with, "It's all about you my beloved brothers. Let your true voice rises in the Legislative Council." At that time I was only 14, I didn't give much attention to politics. I only wanted my father to win in the elections and to be a member in the Palestinian legislative council. He wanted honestly in government, to remove any corruption or conspiracy from the overall Palestinian case for statehood. I believed in that dream.

This was a dream, however, that never come true. We were told that the elections had many violations. One of the main political parties wanted to win the majority of the seats in the council to ensure their domination and control over the political life in Palestine – keeping political power in their hands. I'll never forget the disappointment on my father's face at the end of election day. My dad knew at that moment he would not win. He knew that there was a political game to manipulate the elections for the benefit of Fatah party, the main political party in Palestine.

My father didn't give up hope. Ten years later, in 2005, during the second uprising, the Palestinians successfully managed to hold presidential and parliamentary elections. Even though he didn't nominate himself, he kept his belief in the importance of individual engagement in shaping the political system. I remember that day during the second presidential elections when I went to Jenin to visit my family. I arrived in the late afternoon. My Dad was at home, back from work. He asked me if I registered my name in the registry of the elections. I said, "Yes, I did. He replied, "I voted. Did you my dear?" I said "No, I didn't have time to vote yet" My dad replied back to me, "Everyone should participate in the elections. No matter what the results are. Even if you want to keep your poll ballot empty. You should go and do your duty." So that's what happened. Even though the polling centers were about to close, my Dad took me by his car to the polling center. When I finished, he asked me to keep my registry card so I'll be able to vote for the Parliamentary elections that took place one year later.

I didn't know at that moment that in some how I'm going to be involved in the electoral process of the Parliamentary elections, at that time I was new graduate from BirZiet University in Ramallah with a BA in English Literature and Translation. In 2004 after the death of Yaser Arafat founder of PLO "Palestinian

National Authority" and the taking over of presidency by Mahmoud Abbas 2005 the Palestinians were ready to start their second Parliamentary elections. The Palestinians at that time were in a good place of their mission in establishing the preliminary basis of a Palestinian state that started with Oslo accords coming through establishing ministries, governmental institutions, more civil society organizations and NGO's all of which could miraculously stay standing despite all Israeli invasions and military actions against the civil institutions during the second Intifada 2000-2007. In 2003 the third draft of the Palestinian constitution was released and the efforts have been drifted to amending the Palestinian Basic Law which is a temporary constitution of Palestine.

In 2006 I joined the Canadian observation mission for the Legislative Council Elections. I worked with them as an interpreter where I had to escort two of the observers in the Nablus governorate. In this mission I joined the observers for one week before the day of elections. We did field visits to the polling centers in the villages that were scheduled for us. The purpose was to ensure that the centers are fully prepared, equipped and empty of any political signs for any party. I remember while we were visiting one of the polling centers which was basically a local school when the observers noted that the picture of late president Yasser Araft shouldn't be hang on the wall as it symbolizes Fatah party. These elections were really fair and honest I witnessed the counting of the votes with the two observers while we spent the night at one of the main polling centers in Nablus city to observe the process. Although I didn't have the chance to vote in these elections as I'm registered in Jenin governorate and should vote there but I don't regret it as I was able to participate in a democratic experience and had the chance to spent the day of elections visiting the polling centers with the two Canadian observers translating for them. This was a unique experience for the Palestinians who are still unable to do regularly as it should be due to internal conflicts between the two main parties Fatah and Hamas. My aspiration now is to witness and participate in a third round of Presidential and Parliamentary elections where the Palestinians will be able to conduct free and fair elections as they did in 2006. All the Palestinians should work together and dedicate their efforts to towards building a better place for the coming generations to live in a free, independent and a worldwide recognized Palestinian state living in just peace.

I am still listening to my cousin, in my grandmother's house, as I think about my family's history, their continual involvement in attempting to support Palestinians and the Palestinian cause. My grandmother's witnessing the displacement and struggle of Palestinians in the face of Israel's statehood. The courage of my father to join in military struggles to do his duty towards his country. His continued courage in running for political office. His belief in Palestinians ability to govern themselves, to gain back their homeland. I reflect that memories are occurring in my grandmother's living room, where we all sit, as men and woman, talking laughing and having serious conversations together – an atmosphere which is not very common for other families in my town, who are more conservative and don't feel comfortable with the idea of men and women setting together.

I sit back, reflecting upon my responsibility to participate in this history of struggle and courage, ultimately deciding to step forward to apply for the education program that will take me so far away from home.

And I look forward to that moment when I can return home, celebrate those, warm lovely weekend nights at my Grandmother's house, and carry forward our family traditions.

Ahmed Abdelhakim Hachelaf

ALGERIA

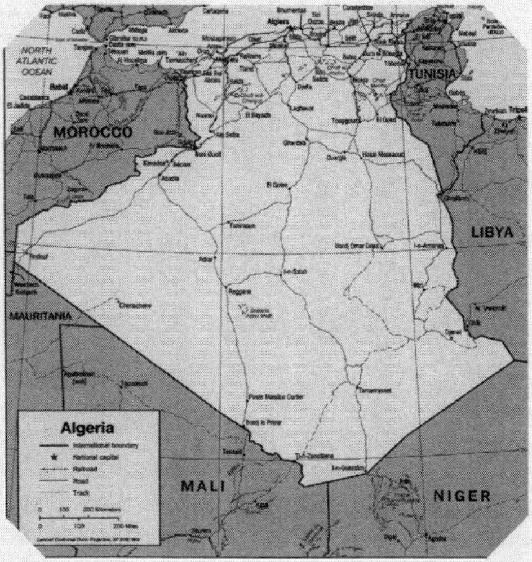

EDUCATING PEOPLE:
A TRUE PANACEA

Algeria, Sweet Home:

My self-portrait

Algeria is located in Northern Africa, having a coastline of 1200 km that borders it with the Mediterranean Sea. It shares borders and cultures with five nations of the Grand Maghreb: Tunisia and Libya to the East and to the West—Morocco, Western Sahara and Mauritania. To the South, it stretches 2000 km bordering Niger and Mali. It is now Africa's first largest country after the division of Sudan covering an area of more than two million square kilometer.

Algeria has a very beautiful landscape. To the North, a very fertile agricultural strip enjoys the excellent climate of the Mediterranean. It is the source of most of the country's food needs. The high plateau strip where I live is a semi-arid area which is located between two mountain ranges. In the south, the Sahara

An extremely beautiful country

Desert spreads for thousands of kilometers; it is arid and sparsely populated but beautifully calm and spacious. Underneath its sands resides the fifth largest reserve of natural gas in the world. The Hydrocarbons industry is the backbone of our economy. Despite these plentiful resources, its people suffer from difficult living conditions, unlike their counterparts in other oil-producing countries. A large proportion of the population is unemployed and for those who receive income, it is very low that it hardly suffices for the basic needs. A small proportion of the population accumulates wealth and is incredibly rich.

In Algeria, our history is even richer than our geography. Algerians have lived a long history full of lessons and calamities that made the people emerge stronger and wiser, for history is the best teacher. We pride ourselves of our glorious war of liberation against the French colonization that had invaded Algeria since 1831. After engaging in scattered confrontations here and there, Algerians learnt that they can only win the war if they are unified, and so they decided to start the National Revolution on November 1st, 1954. It was the start of a bloody war that lasted for seven years in which we paid a million and half a million of our best people to gain the long-awaited protracted liberation. To date, we still live in the shadow of their glories, and the war of liberation emanates a strong sense of national identity.

After political independence, Algerians have to complete their struggle for total independence to this date. As any other emerging revolutionary country, Algeria followed the path of Communism. At that time, the political scene was characterized by a strong hold of a single ruling party namely the National Liberation Front and a strong National Army.

The Algerians continued to take lessons from the best teacher, history, and engaged in many reforms in all sectors. Political liberalization and reforms that opened the political scene to political pluralism were declared after riots in 1988. The following decade was arguably the most tragic and most complex that it is widely known as the 'dark decade'. Over 200,000 people killed, and the Algerians to date are struggling to understand what happened, let alone to understand the lesson behind it.

Algeria and the Arab Spring:

Recently, the Algerians with the rest of the world watched with startling and perplexity, happiness then fear, in this order I guess, the wave of tumults in the region known as the Arab spring. But, unlike the other countries of the region, Algeria was one of the exceptions and no real riots or regime changing demands happened. To my mind, there are many reasons why Algeria has been the exception. First, we had a head start in democracy and freedoms compared to the other countries in the MENA region. We had political pluralism two decades ago. We had also a heritage of freedom of expression that far exceeds the countries around us. The media being critical of the government and strikes and sit-ins are things that can be seen day to day and are tolerated. These assets of freedom of expressions worked as safety-valves that prevented people from rioting. Most of the Algerian people were hungry but at least they were allowed to cry unlike neighboring autocratic regimes who make their people starve and prohibit them from crying, this adding insult to injury. Moreover, there were people in both the political society and civil society who started to make ways into reforms and all the Algerians started to watch this small betterment in all sectors.

The history as an educator was the main factor in the collective conduct of the Algerians distinguishing us with our own unique trajectory, but what about education, and educators as a source of total sustainable reform for the next generation? The problem of most of reforms is that they are top-down. The change in this case is cosmetic and shallow. Even uprisings in the Arab world if not accompanied with educating people will be easily confiscated. Thus, genuineness and sustainability lie in education. I don't feel that this is an exaggeration if I consider it a panacea for all problems yet sometimes the source of all problems.

Education, a panacea or a Poison:

Education in most of our world's countries is not playing the roles it is supposed to play to say the least. Most of the time, education institutions are reflections of the political agendas seek reproduction of the "good citizens", putting people into the same molds, the mold of quietism, passivity and obedience. I guess there is no better description of world's education and media today than Orwell's world trying to tell us paradoxically that war is peace, slavery is freedom, ignorance is strength, questions are disrespectful, memorization is learning, initiative is risky… clearly contradictory ideas and obvious lies, yet, they are trying to make us believe sincerely that this is the Truth.

Like most of my counterparts, and as is the case in many countries, I was raised in an educational system that is characterized by standardization and memorization. I was required to memorize long poems and pieces of prose, and no one really requested me to understand them or analyze them. The poem is what they say it means. I used to get perfect marks when I regurgitated what I received. Students who try to go off the "topic" usually end up buying cigarettes in the streets. But I, with many other good students who used to shut up all the time, remained silent and we ended up in the university auditoriums. I clearly understood that shutting up and being obedient is what made me deserve the appellation of a good student. Thus, I remained a good student.

The focus in schools is on the irrelevant information that does not take the learner very far. It is keeping the learner at the edge of survival and never giving him/her any thought provoking content that may jeopardize his/her comfort or cause him/her to start to worry about anything.

For that, I graduated from the high school resentful of schooling and hoped for a better place in the university that, in my perception at that time, was a place of research and in-depth learning that I thought will render me a scientist in my field. I chose education as I had aspirations to be a perfect teacher.

At the Ecole Normale Superieure, that is the teacher education institute in Algeria, the situation was even worse. The institute not only fails in producing perfect teachers but even plain teachers. Most of these teachers were not able to

In my first secondary education class with friends and teachers

With friends in the secondary school me on the right

teach their subject matters let alone being able to inspire, educate or lead, with the exception of only few who were self-educated. The overall culture of the Ecole Normale Supérieure is characterized by the dominance of teachers. With few exceptions, these Teachers with the capital 'T' dominated the classrooms with their dictations and dictatorship. The teachers hand out their huge handouts and we resorted to the old wisdom of memorizing. Marks were the Weapons of Pass Destruction. The teachers were very revered. They gained our respect and obedience by giving us mean marks. This fact among other factors made the days of my tertiary level very somber and dull if not threatening and insufferable.

In my fourth year at the Ecole Normale Supérieure, along with other colleagues, we decided to make an end to this at least in our circle. We founded a club that had the objective of providing a variety of activities in a stress-free environment for both the students and the teachers. The idea is that all the activities should be run by students for the students. The club organized a wide range of activities including guest speakers, movie shows, study days and debates among other things. The informal supportive atmosphere paved the way to self-actualization and self-esteem to take place by allowing us to be more open and more outspoken. Both students and teachers took part in events and issues related to all aspects of life. This helped on the one hand to mold our personalities and infused us with positive ideas. On the other hand, this encouraged us to have our say, and not passively accept the events around us.

The club started by democratic elections of the board and I was elected as the president. In a short time, we learnt more than what we did from the long hours and days we spent in auditoriums and classrooms. While we enhanced our English through interaction and intensive exposure, we developed most importantly our social and leadership skills as well. The leadership skills such as risk-taking, collaborative work, listening to each other, communicating are highly important

Me in the middle, with the officers and inspiring professors during a Guest-speaker event of the club.

in a highly changing and challenging world. Many among us experienced for the first time the unusual skills of questioning, critiquing and opining.

After graduation, I went to the professional life full of resentment and gratitude. Resentment to the passivity and heteronomy which characterize our educational system, and gratefulness for the English club initiative that helped me develop a lot.

As a teacher, I was told by the curricula writers to teach under the same circumstances. I had the noble mission of participating in producing the "good citizens". It is the same citizenship making that I had gone through in my schooling, a schooling that tended to perpetuate rather than change or challenge the conditions of the world around me.

One of the things that I learned by myself is that good citizenship is not always saying 'yes' but sometimes saying 'No' because that is also one of my duties as a citizen. One of the first 'No' situations that I experienced was during my first year as a teacher. It was a struggle with one of the schools headmasters in my city. He represents all the injustices existent in my society. Yet, he was very revered in my city because he had connections. Connections are the most important factor to transcend in the social ladder and cronyism and nepotism are of the keys of access and 'success'. He was a stout arrogant man who was the director of a neighboring school.

Year in year out, his school achieved excellent rates of success in the baccalaureate and this is thanks to his 'strategy'. His strategy consists in expelling any student that he thinks are not going to succeed in the baccalaureate. His ultimate objective was to have a great success rate in the Baccalaureate in order to get the promotions and the prizes that the directorate of education offered for the best directors. Thus, he put pressures on the teachers to give mean marks for all students who were not likely to contribute in the success rate. He tried to do that on the expense of the poor children. I used to know of one of those victims of this headmaster. He was an intelligent student who passed his primary year with excellence and merit, yet he was expelled because the director thought that they could not be sure that this student is going to succeed. Thus, he was not given the chance to go through his final year, and he was expelled from the school. To date, this student sells vegetables in thc local market.

The situation was insufferable yet he was getting recognition from officials as a very successful school principle. The poor parents of the expelled students used to come to the school to beg this HEAD master to give their children a chance to repeat the year in HIS school—but no way. Moreover, almost every day in my city we used to hear of his ethical and corruption scandals. These parents thought they could do nothing about that or rather the local culture made them think they could nothing to do about that. Many parents were desperate.

It was that sweltering summer day that I decided to do something about that. I was invigilating the national middle school exam and we had to go to his secondary school for lunch breaks. He was snobbishly circulating in the school canteen and talking with teachers who came from all around the city. He gave them orders about where he wanted them to sit, and in a very insulting manner he told a teacher to stand up and change his seat. I did not really manage my emotions and I stood up and told him to be respectful. I used really bed language and while I only used a few curses, I don't regret using them to this date. I then stood up on one of the lunch tables and started speaking about this man's corruption and him sinning against our kids. I asked the teachers to abstain from eating and to go out of the canteen, that we can write a petition against him. Almost every teacher was mobilized into action because they all were thinking the same about him but did not know how to confront him. Sometimes, we think we are too weak to change something, but we forget we can at least say it, 'No'.

We went out and wrote a petition together. We threatened to go on strike and never work in the afternoon. The situation was very crucial for him, and he started apologizing. Officials from the directorate of education came. They tried to calm us down and we finally accepted his apology. The next day, three newspapers were writing about the incident and about his conducts. Two years later, he got a promotion..

The Talk-and-Chalk is not the Perfect way of teaching:

One of the other first things I did after getting the job placement in the same high school that I studied in is establishing an English club there. The English club proved even more successful. Adolescent students were full of energy and full of enthusiasm. I was happy to see my students develop their communication skills, linguistic skills as well as leadership capabilities and strengthen their ties with each other in an astonishing speed. Examples of the activities organized include: intramural contests, interscholastic contests, students-student debates, excursions, guest speakers, theatrical plays, a newsletter, a magazine, celebrating national days, exhibitions, environmental campaigns, poverty fighting projects, modeling the City Council and modeling the United Nations, among other things. All of these activities gave students the chance to engage in the issues and the challenges

Me with my students

With my students, teaching them in the open-air

of their communities. The structure of the club is horizontal in nature and the decisions taken within the club were democratic and participatory.

It is my belief that students should develop these very skills to function as autonomous individuals and future leaders. Educating people is not something we do for the students but with them in a way that challenges established thoughts and practices. The desired result is having empowered citizenry which participates in governance productively and critically. This can be done to a large extent in frameworks such as clubs and associations. This relationship between the schools and universities should be strengthened.

In my context, the initiative of the club was not easy to construct. There were cultural and psychological constraints for what we wanted to do. One of the challenges I got I was lacking the frank authority to do so. The system that is created doesn't support usually independent activities and risk-taking. The lack of material conditions was another concern, and administration not only failed in providing the materials but were resistance to such an initiative altogether. On the other hand, resistance of others to new ideas and new roles is believed to be a human habit. People don't tend to systematically surrender to whatever they find new. Going against the grain is not always welcome but leaves a good impression if it succeeds.

Such initiatives are affected by the way people construe the role of both the teacher and the students. Teachers who go beyond the usual job of the traditional teacher may be rejected, at least for a while, by society. Moreover, traditional upbringing in most of the regional cultures in Algeria, and elsewhere, inhibit showing initiative and taking responsibility. This causes people to be cautious about being in the limelight and in the front line for purposes of modesty and safety.

Three years later, I returned to the university to engage in research. At the department of English in the University of Algiers, I learnt a lot of things from great teachers who taught me the value of modesty and openness. As a magister student, I learnt that students' contributions must be valued and recognized, and that critical thinking and analyzing are among the higher thinking skills that must be tapped in any educational setting. I was inspired by teachers who were themselves fighting battles against the status quo of the Algerian university.

The Core-requirement, Leadership:

As a researcher, I conducted a my thesis on "The Leadership Apprenticeship in the Algerian Education System". Leadership apprenticeship is my understanding of leadership as a process of leaderful practice in the classroom. What I called the leadership apprenticeship is the operation of the transmission of leadership from the teachers to the learners. All participants in the educational process be they headmasters, teachers and even students have the right and the ability to lead.

It seemed to me that leadership can be likened to job apprenticeship where the apprentice learns a skill from a skilled employer. Like professional apprenticing, leadership is a set of skills to be learned and it is through doing that the learner acquires these skills. In addition, the learners apprentice the skills by following a role model and an experienced example in front of them. Thus, the leaders should establish a space of leadership apprenticeship by providing the opportunities for learners to practice leadership and share the decision-making, closely monitoring their teacher's way of behaving and bearing, aiming at self-discipline and self-directed learning.

Undoubtedly, the teacher has the leadership capacity to pass on leadership skills to his/her learners in order to empower them to lead successful productive lives. The aim at the end is the autonomy and leadership of the students. The idea came from the practical involvement in the club and my resentment of the teachers who undemocratically lead and dominate in their classes. My belief is that, by having a democratic teacher leader in front of them, students tend to learn the leadership skills of their teachers either by influence or by the amount of responsibilities and trust put on their shoulders as well as the activities that aim to develop those skills.

The ultimate goal of education should be bringing up leaders who practice their citizenship in a productive way. The goal at the end should not be coping with the demands of the world, because anyone can do that, but rather the goal should be changing and challenging that world, aspiring to make the world possibly—but our countries first—a better place.

All that I have been doing is to try and make some modest changes inside an educational system. A system that the least that can be said about it is that it is a captive of its political scene. Education becomes an agenda that has the objective of political quietism. It is no secret that the kind of individual that is produced by educational institutions is most of the time based on the vision of the politicians. The politicians' main concern is to focus on the skills that do not take the learners very "far". They are the skills of memorization while keeping silent, being obedient, disciplined and oblivious, rather than thinking critically and dialogue openly.

Education is not about programming people but opening their minds on independent thinking and action.

Shadin Hamaideh

JORDAN

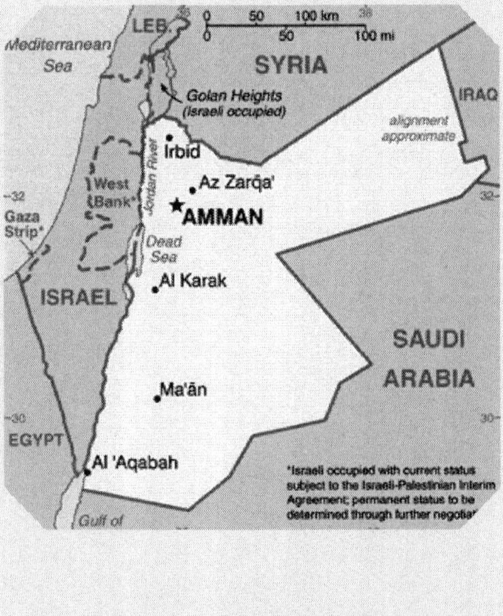

YES, WE ARE SEXY FOLKS!

"True, we didn't have a revolution, nor did we have any civil war, nor do we have a drop of oil; yet we are as sexy and interesting as other countries." I said that, with all the enthusiasm there is in me, when I was once asked to introduce my country, Jordan. Located in the heart of the Middle East, Jordan is a small country with a collectively big heart, a country of no extremes, never really taking sides or standing on harsh ends of political or cultural matters. To me, we are a country of stability and equilibrium, not only internally but also in the region. We are a sanctuary. People come to us to seek peace and security, and this creates the balance which is much needed in a region that is, literally, on fire.

Jordan is also a very humble country; its people are very welcoming; visitors or newcomers are hosted so well that they call them family. In Jordan, people come from different origins, different backgrounds. They are all Jordanians by passport and by name, but in their origins they are not Jordanian. This creates a vague national identity and people seem to misunderstand how to love their country. They misunderstand the meaning of good citizenship. Whenever Jordan is in a football match against another country, if we win, people go outside and cheer like crazy. They block the streets dancing. They stay out all night carrying the Jordanian flag, wearing the *hattah*, our red and white scarf, and they make a really big fuss over it. You feel like everybody is Jordanian. But then they go back home. They deny the rights of women. They don't work hard in their jobs. They rarely volunteer. They don't follow rules. They don't believe in accountability.

So in Jordan, people will say they feel Jordanian, but they still truly identify as a citizen of their country of origin. In the United States, for example, when you ask an American who looks Chinese, "Where are you from?" he's going to tell you, "I'm American." He will never come to the part that he's from China until you really press him and ask him, "Where are you *originally* from?" But, in Jordan, you don't have to ask, "Where are you *originally* from?" Even if they have Jordanian passports, people would still state their country of origin, denying the fact that they were born and raised in Jordan and that Jordan has been a very hospitable home for them. This really breaks my heart, because when you don't feel that this is your country, you will never work hard for it. You will never volunteer. You will never have a decent job and be productive in it. You will never care for that country, and you will never feel that you're a citizen, a *good* citizen that belongs to that country, not only in words but also in actions - genuinely doing good for that country.

People don't consider themselves Jordanian for many reasons. It has to do with them being originally from other places in the world, and it has to do with the country itself. It has to do with how many of their rights are granted, how accountable they are, and how rewarded they feel. I sometimes feel that we are given the shell of the egg in terms of rights, not the egg itself; we tend to stay on the surface when it comes to our rights. No one can claim that we do not have the right to education, freedom of speech, health care, fair trials, employment, free elections and all the rest of the package of human rights. However when you look closer you find that we have the titles but not the body of the rights.

That's one factor of not being able to practice good citizenship. You want to become part of a country when you feel that you contribute to it and that country really contributes back to your life. I put in my share and expect the country to put back in its share towards a better life of its citizens. So I have my duties as a citizen but I also want to know my rights will not be crushed. I want to know if I do well, I will be appreciated, to know if someone makes a mistake, they will have to pay for it.

I think we, as Jordanians, have so much potential. We have a beautiful country and we have people with great minds. I believe one of the main treasures of Jordan is its people. We have to invest in people; we have to work on utilizing this resource and encourage people to contribute back to the country. We deserve a better life! We deserve to have good education, to have a secure job, to be able to open up businesses and know where they are going, and to know people will be punished when they make mistakes. We deserve to grow our good citizenship. And we deserve to have all of the above granted equally to all Jordanians, not taking into consideration their origins, their social status, their titles, or how big their bank accounts are.

My own journey to becoming actively engaged in these issues came through – and remains my education. I come from a family that thinks education is sacred; a family that thinks that getting proper education is more important than bread! I believe this has been a result of my father being born right after his father died, who also lost his mother at the age of ten. He had to move from one relative's house to another. He had to walk to a public school in Kerak for two hours every day, back and forth. Finally, he graduated with a very high average and went to university in Egypt to study engineering. From this he learned that had he not worked hard on getting the proper education, he would've been a shepherd.

He encouraged my mother to study law, even though she was 40, a working mother of five children. He had pushed her in every way towards this goal; a goal she so passionately longed for since she was very young. She couldn't study law in Jordan back then, as there was no school of law, so she settled for a different major, but had that dream of becoming a lawyer ever since, a dream she finally realized years later. Once when I was driving her to the airport to travel to New York City to represent Jordan in an important conference in the UN related to human's and women's rights, she told me, "Being the successful lawyer I am now is all because of your father's encouragement and trust!" She was very grateful to my father being the man he is, always helping her reach new levels. She is, herself, a very ambitious woman and my inspiration in being a good citizen in all sorts of ways—being an active member of society and wanting, always, to contribute more.

Influenced by my father, an engineer, and his belief in a good education, I also studied engineering. However, I have never worked for a single minute in engineering. It's a long story. Many of us in Jordan, study whatever their average gets them, not what they really want to, as mostly, we don't know what we want until a very late stage. In addition to the fact that students are not aware of the different fields of study, students poorly relate those fields to the job market or future careers or businesses due to irrelevance in education and the lack of practical and hands-on experience at an early age.

So, when I graduated, like any clueless graduate, I looked for a job, any job! So I became a teacher! I believe that one of the most rewarding jobs in the world is teaching. To me, the power that you get when you stand in a classroom, and how much impact and influence you can have on students is tremendous. But in our country, teaching is really underestimated—they say if you don't have a job, you go teach—it's the job for jobless people. Although I was a very good teacher during the four years of my teaching career, I decided to shift gears. I needed a career that expresses my aspirations better. I needed to find a career that aligned with my passion.

I knew I wanted to give back to the community. I knew I wanted to really make a difference but didn't know how back then. So I went and earned an MBA. I thought this would give me an insight into the business world or perhaps a good shift from the combination of engineering and teaching. And it did! A colleague of mine in the MBA program was the CEO of INJAZ, a non-profit organization focused on entrepreneurship, leadership, and civic education, who encouraged me to apply for a job there. I did and I was hired. Since then I have been a member of INJAZ family, believing in their mission and working with youth, inspiring and empowering them through different programs.

This was the moment where I found my passion. I thought this is the path I'm going to take for the rest of my life. I'm going to work and focus on good citizenship, working to enable folks to see what it means to act as a citizen through helping people contribute voluntarily to the country, either through social enterprises or through starting a business. Get them to really feel that they are contributing to Jordan through whichever project they choose, making them feel "this is home to me."

I know that if you feel that you belong to a country, you will do good, you will follow the rules, you will work hard, you will tag along with the system and you will definitely feel home. Everyone would like to take pride in what they do, would like to be successful and recognized. If we can grant this to the youth in Jordan through civic education, particularly in social entrepreneurship, I believe that we can tackle the issue of good citizenship. Through the different projects of social and business entrepreneurship, people will feel proud of their contributions and achievements in the country and they would continue to work hard and feel the joy of being a true Jordanian.

I have seen youth working so hard on projects alongside their very well established mentors. I have seen them make a difference in many lives. I have seen them take pride in what they do and do all of that out of love and passion to Jordan. People will work hard when they feel that they are being held responsible and when they believe that they can make a difference. This is why I believe that entrepreneurship is an effective tool in fortifying good citizenship and in steering people towards the one good goal intended.

Like Martin Luther King, my favorite leader in American history, I have a dream, a dream of a better Jordan, a Jordan with utilized energy and knowledge, a Jordan with true democracy and good citizenship, a Jordan with involved people in the decision making process, a Jordan that values its people as they are its national treasure, a Jordan living equality in opportunities, a Jordan with an active and eager civil society, a Jordan with accountability as a core practiced value. I have a dream of a better Jordan.

Mohammed Masbah

MOROCCO

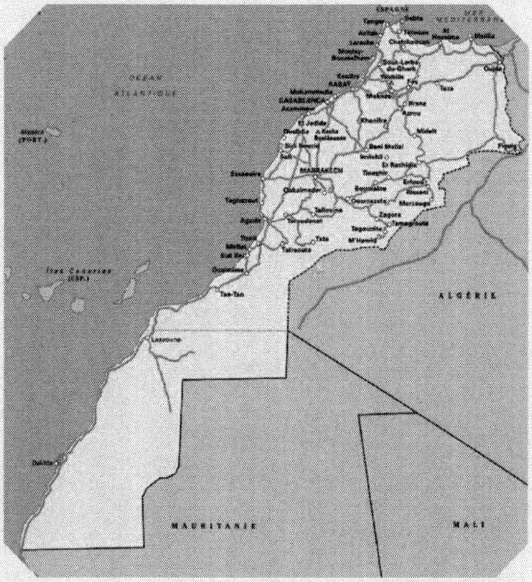

QUE DU BIEN!
AMBITION, CAPACITY, AND MILIEU: KEYS TO SUCCESS

My country: The Time, Place and People

I was born In Oujda, a medium city in the north east of Morocco, close to the Algerian border. For this reason, many Moroccans consider us as Algerians. Morocco is a country situated in North Africa, close geographically to Europe. It has a long historical relationship with the African continent, and it is considered a member of the Arab world for centuries. Morocco has cultural diversity with about five sub-cultural regions: the *Rif* in the North, it is at the intersection between the Mediterranean Sea and Atlantic and it has quite a specific culture which is close to Andalusia and Arab culture, and also a distinct Berber dialect called *Tarifit*. In the central part of the country, we have Fes and Meknes and imperial cities, the centre of the kingdom for centuries. In the East, we have the oriental region, from Oujda to Figuig in the South, it is a semi-desert region with limited natural resources. The south of Morocco is characterized by *Sahraoui* culture and the west coast characterized by concentration of population and wealth, but more individualistic.

In the Middle Ages, Morocco was a great nation with unlimited borders Southern France in the North, to the river of Senegal in the South, to Carthage in Tunisia in the East, to the Atlantic Ocean in the West. These historical and geographical parameters gave to the Moroccan personality a feeling of extension in time and space and potentiality to re-live the golden ages of Moroccan civilization in a new context of the 21st Century. Its geostrategic position as the crossroads of three continents put it under the political and cultural influence of its environment, a certain level of connection with other cultures, which make people in a predisposition to be more open-minded to change and to experience new things.

Politics

Politically, Morocco is a monarchy. The king still remains at the heart of the political system. However, there is a growing call for a constitutional monarchy. For a long time, government was appointed by the king in his own willingness. It was called the "Government of King's Majesty" and during the period after independence, there was a conflict between the opposition and the monarchy in the period of the King Hassan II. This led to a split between them which reached its peak in 1965 when the king declared the case of Exception/*Halate Istithnae* and the king's monopolization of all power. There were two failed coup d'états in 1971 and 1972, and in 1975, the king lifted the exception to power. The situation started to change in the 1990s, related to international changes such as the collapse of the Berlin Wall and the Communist Bloc and also because of local challenges related to the bad economic situation caused by a drought that lasted for a decade, and also to the failure of the effects of the Structural Adjustment Program imposed by the World Bank during the 1980s and 1990s. All of these factors threatened Moroccan economy. In 1996 there was a political opening when King Hassan II made constitutional reforms and appointed Abdurrahman Yousouffi from USFP (opposition) to form a government. Some analysts think that was a preparation for the transition of the throne to his son, Mohammed VI. Since this Mohammed VI came to power, he tried to show a different profile than his father has. He tried to show that he is close to people. He personally inaugurated several activities and institutions like the change in Family Code in 2003, the creation of the Equity and Reconciliation Commission in 2004, which is a Moroccan human rights and truth commission created in order to reconcile victims of human rights abuses, such as torture and atrocities committed by Makhzen (the governing elite) during the Years of Lead, with the State. But since the terrorist attacks in Casablanca in 2003, there was a political and human rights withdrawal. The parliament signed the Terrorism Law and under it they arrested thousands of people. The Ministry of the Interior intervened in the internal affairs of the PJD (opposition in that time) and demanded them to not participate in all communal districts but restricted it to only 19% of the overall districts. The political regression reached its peak in 2007 and 2008. These two years witnessed the dissolution of two Islamist political parties al-Badil al-Hadari and al-Umma as well as the rise of the Party of Authenticity and Modernity (PAM) under al-Himma (close friend of the King and Former Minister of the Interior). Even though PAM had not existed during the 2007 elections, al-Himma was quickly able to amass the largest parliamentary bloc as deputies defected from various other parties. In 2011, Morocco ranks 119 in the Democracy Index, released by the Economist Intelligence Unit (a private business) that measures the state of democracy in 167 countries, and 80 among 183 countries around the world, in the Corruption Perceptions Index released by Transparency International. There is also a high level of poverty and illiteracy. About 20% of the population is in extreme poverty and another 20% in vulnerability. Therefore, around 40% of the population live in a difficult situation which comes to about 14 million people. At that same 40% rate is the percentage of illiterate people. However, there is a huge gap in the distribution of wealth. 10% of the richest people have half of the wealth in Morocco, and the rest have the other half. The disparity between people leads to many social troubles. People would feel that they made a lot of effort to get a small amount of money to survive, while there are some people who do not make any effort who have a lot of money. This leads to a feeling of uselessness, injustice within society, social class hatred.

This triangular model of authoritarianism, corruption and ignorance (illiteracy), is a real threat toward real human development which needs hard work to shift toward a more just society. At the same time, there are some opportunities. We have a high level of young people; 65% of the society is under 35 years, so we have a lot of young people that could participate in development. It's a gift we should use it in a good way.

Religion

Morocco is a Muslim society. 99% of people are Muslims, with a small Jewish minority, and some non-Moroccan Christians. Religion plays an important role in people's lives. It is one of three unifying things of the Moroccan Nation; we say: "Allah (God), Nation, and the King." Even if there are differences among people in their perceptions and practices concerning religiosity, people, in general, feel that they are faithful. All of them believe in God and they believe that religion is one part of their lives, and it connects them to each other. Though, the level of regular religious practices is lower, especially among the young population, according to some sociologists' field research, religious practice is steadily increasing compared to 20 or 30 years ago. Moroccan religious attitudes are moderate. Even though 99% of the population is Sunni Muslim, there is an interfaith cohabitation. This is protected by religion itself and also by law. In the Quran there is a verse which translates as: "There is no compulsion in religion" (Surah 2: 256). Also, the constitution and law protect people of other faiths to practice their religion freely. And one important feature of the Moroccan religious landscape is that it is quite homogenous. It is mainly defined as Sunni Muslim with a Malikite Jurisprudence. There is no confessions as other Arab countries have. Also, people succeed in developing a culture of dialogue within society and sectarianism is marginal.

As the state monopolized the interpretation of religion, it gave itself the right to accept or reject any other way of interpreting religion, which means it restricted the way to interpret religion, from inside. In Islam, religious scholars are the heirs of the prophets. They are the people who are entrusted to preserve the faith of people and interpret accurately religion. They have the tools to do so. It is not a clergy, a class which justify the status quo. They should not be a state apparatus, like it was in Christendom in the Middle Ages, but rather a part of society, and emerge from the internal dynamics and be self-organizing. So, religious scholars should organize themselves by themselves by making internal election of the body that should lead them and take decisions from people who are pious and strong to say the truth in front of the most authoritarian ruler. They must belong to society, not to the state. They should be paid from the Endowment/ *Waqf* which belongs to the people. This independence from any political or state's influence will give them strength to defend un-biased religious interpretation; they can be a counter-power to the symbolic violence of the state. It is a fourth (or fifth) power. It is considered as a pious civil society. They are the consciousness of people. Their role is not only protecting the faith of people but also to be a part of people to defend their rights, to emancipate them from oppressors, to be "God's Slave" and not a human's or anything else's slave. For example, in Egypt, during the revolution, some of Al-Azhar University (one of the oldest religious universities) scholars participated in the protests against Mubarak's regime with the people.

My City

Even if Oujda city belongs politically and socially to the Kingdom of Morocco, people in this city maintain important ties with Algerians. The dialect and customs are close to Algerians, especially between east of Morocco and West of Algeria. My father was born in Mascara, in the west of Algeria. My grandparents and uncles lived there for about 25 years until 1975 when the political relations between Morocco and Algeria deteriorated, and then they returned to live again in Oujda. And I remember when I was young, we hosted a lot of Algerians in my grandparent's house, and we visited Algeria before the borders was closed in 1994, after which the situation changed, and people felt frustrated because of the destruction of their source of income which was based on commerce and tourism with Algerian visitors.

Oujda was perceived to belong to the "Useless Morocco." It is a term that was used by the French occupation when it divided Morocco in two parts: "useful" and "useless" Morocco. From Taza to the Eastern borders, the region was considered "useless" and from Fes to the West side of Morocco, it was considered as "useful" due to natural and social factors. Western Morocco has a moderate climate, abundant agriculture, mineral resources, and is in close proximity to the capital. People in Oujda felt always that they are distant from the "centre"/ the capital, Rabat, and the economical capital, Casablanca. People of the "centre" were considered by Oujdis as "Gharbi", i.e. westerners, in both sides, geographically and culturally. People in Oujda stereotyped "Ghrabas" (plural of Gharbi). They said *Ghrabas* don't have good values and they are materialistic and their families are destroyed like Western countries and also they perceived them as ego-centric caring only about themselves and not about all of the citizens. They were thought to not care about "Useless" Morocco. For this reason, Oujdis developed a kind of "independent" mindset even if they feel that they belong to Morocco, but they are critical of its negligence.

Childhood

I had a diverse experience. There's no single factor that influenced my ideas. There are different backgrounds and different factors; it's the combination of all these experiences. If we want to organize my life, in order of their relative importance, we can say: family first, then school, and then civic society, in which I work, and then the other factors.

My family is considered as conservative and also open minded. They are attached to the traditions and values of the society. They taught me to be authentic and modern at the same time. When I was 10 and 16, I went regularly during free time and in summer to the mosque to memorize the Quran, and also to a French Institute to learn French language and culture. I did both of them without feeling a contradiction in my behaviour; there is no contradiction between preserving your own identity and being open to the world. Identity gives you a strong feeling of belonging but it shouldn't be an obstacle to seeing the complexity of the world or not to learn from other regardless of who they are. One has a mind to distinguish between what is good and what is bad from ones own culture and from the other culture and one can take the best of both.

Even if there are some similarities between my paternal and maternal family, there are also differences. In political choices, some cousins and uncles in my paternal family are more sympathising to the PJD (Party of Justice and Development), which is a Political party with an Islamic Background, and that is due maybe to the influence of my father. My maternal family voted for some local figures more than a specific ideology, and that is due maybe to the influence of my grandfather who is a notable in the city. However, he changed some of his political ideas, and he is now sympathizing to the PJD because he thinks they are more honest than other politicians he tried before.

My father has always been a person that affected my life, and gave me a lot of insights about meanings in life, how to behave with others, and especially to be independent. He was my father and Teacher of Life. He always told me to rely on myself, to do things by myself. Not only that, but he did some exercises and tests for me since I was child to be independent from him. He always inspired me with his deep vision, how to be moderate in my ideas, and how to be patient to get what I want.

There is a good story to be narrated. When I was 5 or 6 years old, my father sent me to my grandparents' house alone by public bus. He talked to the man responsible for collecting the tickets on the bus to drop me off in the Medina (downtown) Station, which is the closest station. After that, I had to walk about 300 feet alone from the bus station to my grandparents' house. Then, he called my uncle to be sure that I arrived. This experience was wonderful. From this small experience, I felt that I could do things without being attached to my father. It was freeing. It is an example of his way of teaching me to be independent in my life. When we talked about some problems I had in school or in life in general, he'd say to me: "Can you think in another way? Do you have other alternatives? What are the options you have?" When I replied: "I can't. It's impossible." He would respond, "Never say I can't. Try it again, do it, and if you fail you see another way to do it, and never stop in the first step. You can do it. Just believe in your own capacity," He tried to teach me some Quran verses: "Are those who know equal to those who do not know?" Only they will remember [who are] people of understanding" (Surah 39:9). It means you should make your effort to learn things, and people who have knowledge (scholars) are much better than those who don't have it. This doesn't mean that I was not affected by some people. On the contrary, there were a lot of people who I was affected by, most of them were local figures who gave me insights and inspiration in my life.

My grandfather was more than 101 years old when he died in 2001. He was a pious man, full of wisdom and love. Everybody loved him, especially the kids. During the last years of his life, he lost his biological eye, but still maintained his third eye, insight (foresight) and deep beliefs. He always prayed for me. Also, my old uncle, who is now in the position of my grandfather, loved me so much, and he always gave me this pure image of love, happiness, and wisdom.

My home was never empty from guests. Every day we had friends of my father who came from everywhere of the world. Most of them were intellectuals and sometimes they were political figures. Even if we had a lot of guests, my mother was always happy to cook for them. I don't know what motivated her to do it, but it made her happy even though it was not easy to cook all the time for those people. She was never angry or tired by doing what she was doing, even if she didn't have someone to help her. But these moments with guests were a great opportunity to share ideas, hear how the elders talk, and how intellectuals think about life. My father was wise. He gave me the choice to stay with them if I wanted, and always I accepted to participate in those events—sometimes because there was good food, sometimes because of the importance of the guest, and sometimes because I needed to be "correct" socially. When I was 10 years old, I wrote a small piece, a story that my imagination created. It was about an experience I lived. It was common for me to write pieces and poetry. As there were many intellectuals who came to our home, he told me one day to read what I wrote and they loved it, told me I would have a bright future.

In Oujda, private school was not popular. It was reserved for rich and privileged people. All my studies were done in public school. I have never been in the private one, only for some extra courses in the high school in mathematics and physics. I was always in competition with other students. I wasn't always the first of the class. Sometimes I was the first in participation, and activities in the class. It means that I participated and talked, but in results I didn't get the highest score in the class. In general, I am a person who asks a lot of questions, every day, and one of my family members told me I talk a lot because I ask "Why is that like that and not like that?" "What's that?" "Why?" "How?" "Can you explain to me?" Many people get bored by my questions, but I always ask. My father was the person who answered me about a lot of things, but other people don't have this willingness to answer, especially in our society, it's not easy to accept all the questions of young people like me. But I had this passion of asking questions a lot.

Since the early age of eight, I participated in several NGO's activities, conferences, camping, to helping poor people, homeless and infirmary. We went there to give them food, to give them clothes, etc...It was voluntary work that we did every time and my father and my mother were active in that charitable work and my home was always open for guests and for poor people and for people in need. It was something which I lived since my childhood and yes, that was a part of my life. When I was young I thought that it's their own fault they were poor, but after attending high school and university, I started to think of the structured injustice in society. Poor exists because there is an imbalance in distribution of wealth that is due to the monopolization and concentration of wealth and power in the hands of few people. So to fight injustice and poverty you should return back the justice, i.e. you should fight to make a divorce between wealth and power.

First Political Experiences

I spent 20 years in my city of birth before I left in 2006 to finish my studies in Sociology in Mohammedia for my bachelor's degree and then in Rabat for a master's degree and PhD.

During this period of my life, I had a diversified experience. I met many people from different backgrounds, adopted, changed, and sustained many ideas and behaviours related to many factors, internal and external.

I was raised in a politicized environment. My father was an active member in several NGOs in Morocco. He is a famous personality in our city. He is well respected by people of the city as one of the most honest professors of philosophy in Oujda high schools. My first political participation was in 1997 in the electoral campaign of a father's friend. I participated as a monitor, not as a real participant, but my first engagement in politics was in 2002, when my father was running for parliamentary elections. He was the second in the list. He had a great chance to be elected, but as the electoral system is complicated, it makes it hard to win. Our

Me (at left), with three friends: Salmane, Abdellah, and Jawad (from left to right), during the preparations of a conference at the University Hassan II- Mohammedia during the fall 2007.

list got more than double the second candidate, and triple of the third, but the electoral law was not in his favour and unfair. This experience taught me a lot of things. One important thing I learned was the fact that I learned to communicate with all segments of society from "ordinary" people to "elites." Sometimes there were some aggressive people who told me: "How much money did they give you to participate?" or they said "You are still young" or "All candidates are the same." It was a challenge for me to develop strong arguments, but also the best manner to transmit my message to them was to convince them that it's not true that everybody is the same. It was a great experience in a medium-sized city like Oujda. It was an important experience for me to talk with people at that early age of 16 and try to convince them and make them sympathise with causes.

Another experience was during my entrance to university when I was 19 years old in 2005. I was an undergraduate student in economy, and I participated for the first time in the annual conference of Renewal Student Organisation in 2006 at the University Mohammed V in Rabat. For one week, we assisted tens of activities (conferences, debates in open air, side talks, artistic activities…) and we met many intellectuals there.

Transforming from Object to Subject

In fall of 2006, I lived the first strong experience in demand for social justice and claim of our rights. I was a student of Sociology in my first year at the University of Mohammedia, a small city between the capital of Morocco (Rabat) and the largest city (Casablanca). I was a member of a Student Organization which is active in all Moroccan Universities. We organized several activities for students, including organizing conference and open days. We talked to the administration of the faculty for the right of students. My NGO organized at the national level a protest in front of Moroccan Parliament about increasing the value of student scholarships from 150$ to 350$. I personally have never received a scholarship during my undergraduate studies because the government awarded these to poor students, and I did not want to take one when someone else needed it more. Because my father was a professor, and I tried to manage myself since the first year in the university, and he never sent me money since the second year in the university, but I believed with many friends that the scholarship given by the government is so weak and it should be doubled three times to give the support for students during their studies.

We were a crowd of several hundred. I came in the train with some of my friends. We went to the parliament. Then, we started to gather and to organize ourselves. Then, there came one police officer who told us that we were not supposed to have this protests despite the fact that we were a legal organization and had made official demands to organize peaceful protestation. He said that there is a European envoy to the parliament, and they didn't want to see us protesting, and he gave the order to the *Mkhaznia*/ (police) to disperse us, and they used violence. They started with the president of the Organization, and one of my friends tried to help him, but he was also hit on his body.

I was so happy, even if there were batons on our backs. I felt free, and I felt they were weak, and we were stronger even though they used violence against us. I felt that they made me free of being killed or to be hit. The most important lesson I got from this experience was that I got more confidence in myself, and it showed me how important it is to be organized in a group, to make pressure for your claims, and not only as individuals, and how normal citizens could make a difference, and how the claim for your rights is so important to be done by yourself and not waiting for the others to give it to you even if you don't achieve what you want in the beginning but you pave the way for others to do so in the future. In all cases, we were so happy in the night by talking about that, and having the feeling of unity with each other.

Since that time, I was not afraid of the *Makhzen* and I was more confident in the possibility of the change from "within." You should have patience, a good strategy and cooperation with peers to achieve your goal.

My focus in political and social activism in Morocco is on democratization and basic human rights shared by every human in the world. I do this in many ways. Sometimes it is by putting pressure from the street protests. It is an important tool but not enough to get what you need if people don't know their own rights, so I think the most important tool to change is raising awareness and empowering and enlightening people. Since the Arab uprisings started and even before, I tried to work hard to raise this kind of awareness about people's rights by organizing events, conferences, debates, trainings for young people, writing articles, and so on.

In a Conference Analysing the results of the elections of 25 November 2011. From left to right, Mustapha Khalfi: Minister of Communication, Me, Fatima Zahrae Hirate: Political Scientist, Maati Monjib: Political Activist, and historian. Abderahim Maslouhi: Political Scientist.
Date: 28 Nov 2011.

During 2011, I published about fifty articles on various topics in Morocco about how democratization processes progress, the mechanism of authoritarianism to come back and control society, defending our rights as young people, and so on. I published these in very famous newspapers. Most of them are available at the first news Web site in Morocco, Hespress.com, and they were published it, sometimes, on the first page's headlines which gives optimum public debate about several topics, so it was very important for me during the last year to be a part of this debate about human rights, democracy, democratization in my society, and I think the power of the pen sometimes is stronger than the power of tanks. So I believe if you write an article, because I don't believe in violence, that it is one tool that you can change toward a better situation. You should convince people. You should try to explain to them by the easiest and most practical way, convincing them by giving them arguments that are good for them or bad for them to change their situation. You do it by your mouth and your pen. We say in Arabic, *The sword has a stronger impact than the pen*, but I think it's the opposite: *the pen has a stronger impact than the sword* because you can put your sword in my head and never change my mind but I can give you the idea and it's your own effort. This is my philosophy of change: by the best means.

What happened in the Arab World?

There is no doubt that the New Media has had an influence on the Arab Spring movements. Principally, the new social media such as Facebook, Twitter, etc. and the international channels such as Aljazeera have had a great impact. From Morocco to Bahrain, the Arab world has been witnessing the rise of an independent vibrant social media where the Internet citizen engagement is steadily increasing and is expected to attract 100 million Arab Internet users by 2015.[1] It was these social media that were used by the protesters to carry their

[1] Ghannam, Jeffrey. Social Media in the Arab World: Leading up to the Uprisings of 2011. The Center for International Media Assistance, February, 2011, p. 4

discourses and transmit the messages to the wider audience in the Arab world as well as in the whole world. Also, the social networking Web sites were the only accessible way for marginal groups to call their claims and to organize rallies with low costs reaching broad audiences inside and outside their own country, rather than the classical media technologies, like television or radio broadcasts being monopolized by the actual governments. Until now, the Internet has been distant from the governmental control or the state monopoly – it is a "no man's land" media. But some Arab governments and decision makers are going to undertake pressure to make restrictions in Internet use as the Google CEO has warned six months after the beginning of the uprisings that there is a potential increase of Internet censorship after the Arab Spring movements.[2]

What has happened in the Arab world in the end of 2010 and in the beginning of 2011 is not a direct effect of the new media – as some journalists and columnists stated – despite its importance and effectiveness, the changes were generated from the previous political and economical core. Political and social actors have played a significant role by acting, thinking, and feeling about their current situation in the society and about their future. Actors are considered as an ability of individuals or groups, such as class movements, governments, or economic corporate bodies, to "make things happen" within given structural constraints and opportunities.[3] So, in this context of social revolt, actor's claims, under the support of several social categories, some call it "population", for more freedom, dignity and social justice.

---

[2] "Google chairman warns of censorship after Arab Spring." BBC News US&CANADA, 27 June 2011, http://www.bbc.co.uk/news/world-us-canada-13935470

Six actors are central for any analysis of the recent events in the Arab region. In particular, (1) Ch'aabe (Population), (2) traditional opposition (Islamists, leftists, ethnic and cultural minorities, etc.), (3) new youth movements, (4) actual government, (5) armies, and (6) the external factors (Western countries).

The new context of "the Arab Spring" gave the opportunity to the trilogy of (1) the Ch'aabe, (2) traditional opposition (Islamists, leftists, ethnic and cultural minorities…), and (3) the new youth movements, a larger margin of action in its relation with other actors. The last two points are a social product of the influence in post-independence of the public schools which has succeeded social accession of new rural generations. This development in the education (knowledge capital) was not followed by an accumulation of the social influence (social capital); for a long time, they were in a disadvantaged position in accessing the available resources, and therefore, they were marginalised in the participatory decision-making processes.

This development in the educational level, which has produced new established elites coincided with the technological development, which became available for important segments of society deprived from it for a long time. Today, most of the technological products are available in Morocco at the same time as in the developed countries; the new technologies have become cheap and accessible for wider social categories, especially for the educated people, both from rural and urban areas who are now fortified by "formal education" and "technological

---

[3] Rob Stones, structure and agency, in George Ritzer (Edited), THE BLACKWELL ENCYCLOPEDIA OF SOCIOLOGY, 2007, Blackwell Publishing Ltd. p. 4869

development." Today, we can say that the Moroccan youth of the 20th February has, so to speak, the entire world in their hands, out of the control of institutions (State, family…), and they can discover the social reality on their own, i.e. the young generations can be informed about what is happening in other Arab countries via Aljazeera, but also via their Facebook pages which have opened to them a window to the world, and the possibility to "share" comments, ideas, images, videos, and much more with other social media users.

However, even if most of the protesters' demands are political and social, they are also cultural demands such as the recognition of minority rights, freedom of speech and expression, etc. There was an important participation of the ethnical, cultural, linguistic and religious groups in several Arab countries (e.g. Morocco, Egypt, Syria, Bahrain…), which has played a significant role in that momentum, by using several tools, such as demonstrations, petitions, publishing articles, media participation….

Many countries claimed the term "exception" in its official discourse, and it is isolated from the popular protests. That is not true because the "Arab revolutions" is like a storm or an earthquake. You could not predict it until it came, even if the timing is surprising sometimes, but it is "unavoidable" because people in the MENA are not less than other human beings in all the world, thirsty for emancipation.

Is Morocco an exception?

In Morocco, there were official discourse claims so called the "Moroccan exception" which was isolated from the popular protests. But it did not wait longer to release a new impetus in political and social fields. With the emergence of the

20th February Movement, launched just after the collapse of the two regimes in the region, the autocratic regime of Zine El Abidine Ben Ali in Tunisia and Husni Mubarak's regime in Egypt. This movement is not monolithic or homogeneous. To a certain extent, it is a mixture of ideological references, from the radical Left to the radical Islamists, and between them there are independent groups and political partisans, moderate Islamists, Leftists, Berberists, etc. In reality, it is a structureless, leaderless, and heterogeneous group, which was able to recruit the new technologies, especially Internet, for engagement of new protesters, diffusion of their ideas, and organization of rallies.

20 February Movement Protestations

Me (at left), with two friends: Issam (in the middle) and Omar (right), during the protestations of 20 Feb. Movement.

Since the Arab uprising started, I started to think how to be proactive, how to participate in this turning point of history of the region. I was so excited to hear of events in Tunisia and Egypt, and I started to write articles in the famous Web site, Hespress.com, and in these articles I made claims for democratic changes in Morocco, and that it is an unavoidable process. I wrote on January 26th (one month before the 20th February Movement started) an article entitled "In the Path of Tunisia: The Inevitability of Democracy in Morocco" and I wrote:

The inevitability of democracy and the inevitability of the defeat of tyranny, this is the basic conclusion that can be learned from the great revolution fought by the Tunisian people against the authoritarian regime of the Party's constitutional assembly of BenAli, this revolution highlighted that people of the region yearn for freedom, pluralism and democracy. Developmental model which sacrifice of freedom has failed, and if people were provided with food and drink, they will be satisfied and the current situation can be satisfied. (…)

"For Morocco, still is at a standstill, so that the depth of the Moroccan political system could not- unfortunately –turn toward the direction of democracy, which emerged clearly through the failure of the "democratic transition", and the emergence of repercussions in favor of "parties of the State" which against real parties which could threaten the interests of ruling elites, and the abuses practiced by the Moroccan administration in favor of one party against another party."

To have a real democratic transition there must be three urgent steps:

"First: real Constitutional reform, that give large functions to the chief of government, that allow him to be accountable in front of the population, that should necessary pass via democratic methods, which means the respect of the ballot boxes results, and choosing the chief of government from the party that got the 1st place in

the elections. Second: political reforms, by organizing fair and free elections, include all political forces, giving guarantees to not intervene in the results of elections, by creating an independent entity from civil society and judiciary body with the control from international independent observers. Also there is a need to put good laws for elections, by taking in consideration demographic weight. Third: fight against corruption and corrupted, by making accountable all Senior officials, from the highest responsible to a simple parliamentary, and showing all their wealth to people, and prohibiting all high level officials to practice business activities that can lead to abuses their power for their own interests"

Five days after, I wrote another article, in which I said:

The collapse of the corrupted Tunisian and Egyptian regimes - We do not know who will come next – was full of coolness and peace for the peoples of the region and gave them an optimistic change for the better, and at the same time siren to all authoritarian regimes to review their political behavior and avoid anything that might give rise the anger of people.
Based on the Tunisian and Egyptian revolution, there is a basic rule:
Authoritarian regimes fall after breaking the barrier of fear to the people.
Our great people in the Arab world believe that democracy and freedom is their destiny, and that the tyranny determination is to go away.

Since that time I wrote about more than 50 articles in about one year (onc article a week), some of them had an important impact. I felt very happy when I met many people everywhere complimenting my articles. Two moments stand out. One time, I met with Dr. Saad Dine Othmani, before he became Minister of Foreign Affairs, and he told me, I enjoy reading your articles, and we missed it recently, and I heard from someone close to him that he read my articles regularly. Also,

Mr. Driss Azami Idrissi, Minister of the Budget, told me once in front of Mr. Mustapha Khalfi (Minister of Communication), I liked your article, and remarked to Mr. Khalfi: "Did you transmit my appreciation to his recent articles?" I was really happy that people, from normal citizen to top officials, read and enjoyed my articles. Of course, some criticized it, but that was marginal, and I did not pay attention to that.

Me in the middle, with the chief of Government, Mr. Abdelilah Benkirane (right) during a meeting with him in March 3th 2012.

One last word:

Revolution is a long process of changing a system to another system, so young activists should be armed with a strategic vision, defining their goals and principles, practical tools and tactics, patience, and searching peers to share values and cooperate to achieve their goals.

Muna Abbas Ali AlBuloushi

KUWAIT

POLITICAL ENGAGEMENT:
RESPONSIBILITY AND EDUCATION

Kuwait is a really modern country; it has been influenced a lot by Europe and the United States. When you walk in the shops and the malls, it's like you're walking into a mini-America. At the same time it's not one of those countries which you don't see the locals. Wherever you go, whenever you go, you will see Kuwaitis all over the places, walking around. We like outdoor activities, going out and gathering with friends.

Kuwait is really a democratic country and we have, what I believe is, freedom of speech. Almost everyone in Kuwait can express his opinion. It is an Islamic country and we follow the Islamic Law. Yet it is open to other cultures and religions. Women in Kuwait don't have to wear the formal Islamic clothing, they can either wear the scarf or not. People can express themselves in different ways within the tradition and customs of the Kuwaiti society. The royal family ruling Kuwait, are open to different ideas. They give space to people to help them in decision-making and giving them high positions in the country.

Unfortunately, I don't see Kuwaitis know how to deal with the democracy they've been given. They don't know how to use it. Rather, they're using it in the wrong way. For example, we had huge protests in our country about the Prime Minister. The Parliament members shouted, "We don't want him." At the same time they didn't give it time, they didn't wait for a solution to be found. Sadly they broke down the doors of the National Assembly, breaking things inside the building, to show where they stand on the Prime Minister. He was removed and the Ruler of Kuwait assigned someone else. At the same time I don't think that this was a proper way to speak your mind or to show a strong stance. They were impatient. Not educated. To me, education is not a matter of your degree. It's a state of mind. Such actions bring disgrace to the country and distorts Kuwait's image internationally.

Kuwait is witnessing a heart breaking time at the presence. A lot of demonstrations are going on in different occasions for different reason, yet the government is having some modest attempts to modify the flaws in the ministries systems.
In Kuwait, women can vote. Yet they're not voting. In 2005, women had the right to vote and be elected; regrettably they're not using it. I mean, women themselves are fighting each other. In the first round after gaining our political rights, we didn't have any women to win and reach the National Assembly. They all failed. Not a lot of people voted for them, so the ruler assigned two female ministers. In the second round, four women won and in the third round, which was Feb 2012, no women won also. For some reason women are not supporting each other, I don't know why. They don't trust each other. For example, when I asked my female friends wither they're going to participate in the elections. All of them said, "No, we won't waste our time." Then some of them said, "No, there is no one worthy." I said "Okay, there're some well known women, we can vote for them!" But I heard the same thing. "No, they're not worthy. When they get into a certain position, they'll be stubborn, closed minded, jealous. She won't give any chance to other people to work." They have this misconception, which is not necessarily true. Well of course there are some corrupt women, at the same time there are a lot of female candidates who would work hard for the growth of Kuwait and there are a lot of men who are corrupt in my country too.

In the second election of the year 2012, December, three women of the candidates were actually able to win the elections of the National Assembly. You may be wondering about the reason of having two elections for the National Assembly in one year. Two candidates of February 2012 elections filed law cases in the Constitutional Court against some of the National Assembly members of the same round and challenged numbers of the judicial orders which were taken by them. The Amir of Kuwait constitutionally dissolved the National Assembly and issued a sentence of which each citizen can vote for only one candidate instead of four. Some people boycotted the elections because of this sentence and others because they're fed up with it. I strongly believe that boycotting the elections equals quitting, we should be strong and fight the corrupt National Assembly Members by facing them.

We also have people who would take advantage of the differences in the country. All Kuwaitis are Kuwaitis; we all immigrated to this country. There wasn't a Kuwait until 1756. And we only gained our independence from the United Kingdom in 1969. So in our country, we have people who are originally from Iraq, Iran, and Saudi Arabia. We also have huge differences between the dominant religions in our country. The main Islamic doctrines in Kuwait are Sunnis and Shia's. Ignorant people try to take advantage of this difference by creating dissensions to spread distinction among the people of Kuwait. The majority of Kuwaiti nationals are Sunnis Muslims; the minority are Shi'a. Shia are a diverse group. Some are Arab, many the descendants of immigrants from Ash Sharqiyah (Eastern Province) in Saudi Arabia or from Bahrain. Families who moved from the Arabian side of the Persian Gulf to Iran, stayed awhile, and then returned. Others are of Iranian origin, whom often speak Persian as well as Arabic at home and sometimes maintain business or family ties with Iranians across the Persian Gulf. [1]

1 Wikipedia: http://en.wikipedia.org/wiki/Religion_in_Kuwait#citenote-factbook-0

What is great about Kuwait is the ruler himself, HH Sheikh Sabah Al-Ahmed, he never, never recognizes these differences, even in the official government, official papers. We are all treated the same. We are all Kuwaitis.

Now the children are acquiring these bad habits from their parents and focusing on those differences. We had a lot of scandals about Shia's and Sunnis. They would fight each other in public, the National Assembly and everywhere. Everyone is seeing it. Everyone is listening to what they're saying; they're misrepresenting, themselves, their families, the society and our beloved Kuwait. When a famous figure would act or say these things in ignorance, people would follow him. I'm seeing this happening in schools. I'm listening to students accusing each other… "I'm better than you, I'm Shiite," "No, I'm better than you, I'm Sunni…" Or they would say, "I'm better than you financial-wise, or you don't have a lot of floor in back." Ridiculous and small things might affect the society negatively. They may seem like foolish actions yet I consider them as mold eating the society. We have the power, so let's use it. We can educate people around you.

Last year, high school students went to protest against the Minister of Education. They did not want him. They wanted to remove him. He had some decisions regarding their marks, conditions of their graduation and other things they didn't like. So they went to protest, but again they didn't protest in the right way. To protest is to show your point and to make people hear you. You don't have to go violent, you don't have to go with the taboos, with wrong behaviors, but this is what they did. So I can see what happened in the National Assembly affected them because they did the same with the Minister of Education.

I became active because I simply care about everything around me. I love my country. I don't want to see it descending to a low position that's against the distinctive values and Kuwaiti traditions we grew up acquiring from our parents and society. We have a beautiful state. We have beautiful cultures, relations, and customs. All of these are vanishing around us because people are taking advantage of these differences to create problems and then tear this country. Right now, to be something in Kuwait, you need to belong to a certain group. Either a religious doctrine group, or a political group, and even to be a feminist you have to belong to the feminists' group in Kuwait. I don't want to do that – I don't want to be belonging to anyone. I want to be just a Kuwaiti citizen who is trying to do the right thing. This is what I see as being broad-minded, to be accepting of others. For me, being a Kuwaiti means to respect everyone, not being a Shia or a Sunni, not battling against each other. I want Kuwaitis to have patriotism in their hearts and to love their country. That's it. We don't have to show our religious beliefs to be accepted. We don't have to convince anyone that we are a good Shia or Sunni. Whatever you want to do, this is between you and Allah. He will judge you, not humans, not anyone. If you want to be liberal then be but on yourself, you don't have to impose your believes on others.

In Kuwait, I teach English in middle school for girls. I didn't imagine myself as a teacher until I was in the classroom. But I love it. I love it very much. This is what I want to do. I want to educate children. Imam Ali Ibn Abi Taleb – the son in law of prophet Mohammed - said, "Gaining knowledge in one's youth is like imprinting it on a rock, it will always remains." So in my opinion, I think in order to affect everyone in this state, I have to effect the youth first. If the youth were taught in the right way then the next generation will have good beliefs. They will not go breaking down the doors of the assembly. I'm trying to teach them to speak it in the right way; how to affect people and make them hear you by good behavior and speaking appropriately. Verbal and physical violence are not the keys for good citizenship.

My class working on a project about cultural differences

Of course, as a teacher, I had to learn to do this myself before implementing it on others. After two months of teaching, I faced a situation, which opened my eyes. I had the naughtiest twelve-year-old female students; this class was known as the wildest class, and all the teachers of that class were always complaining about those students. But for some reason they liked me. They were listening to me and telling me stories about themselves. Still I didn't see my influence on them until a certain incident. One of the students, Rawan, was punished for misbehaving in the class. When she told me her story I laughed at her and said, "You deserve it." and the rest of the class also laughed at her. The next day she came to me, telling me that her sister fell down and hurt her arm; and instead of helping her, Rawan laughed at her and said the exact same phrase that I said to her, "You deserve it." Just at that moment I realized my mistake: I influence those students, either in a bad or good way. I'm helping to build their personalities with my behaviors! Also, as a woman, I have the responsibility to act in a certain way, to show the girls what they can do.

So now I always try to listen to them and try to explain that being different is not necessary a bad thing. For example, instead of debating with them, I would tell them, "I'm different from you in this area yet it doesn't make me less than you." I try to talk to them as much as I can, and not treating them as kids – they don't want to be treated as kids. They're not kids, after all, they're teenagers. At 13, 14 and 15, they are old enough to understand what's going on around them. Since then, I loved being a teacher and help building young students' personalities.

Remember what Imam Ali Ibn Abi Taleb said, these lessons will remain. They will also go beyond the classroom. Let's say I have a little girl going to school every day and then she goes back home with these good ideas and behaviors acquired in school. Her ideas and behaviors will be transferred to the whole family. Think how many other persons would the parents and siblings affect positively because of that one student. They'll also talk about it to the extended family. This young girl, when she grows up, will have in mind these good civic and political behaviors that she learned and acquired in school. She will be an open-minded mom whom would raise her children with this concept.

Again I have to clarify what I meant by open-minded, because there is this misconception about open-mindedness. Back home, people think that open-mindedness is to be too liberal in the way you're dressed up or to be all Americanized and not meeting the standards of the Kuwaiti society. Open-mindedness doesn't mean that. To me, being open-minded means to accept others whoever the others are. We ARE different from each other — either in gender, education, sex, or in color. Yet we have to accept each other and live in harmony.

Give education a chance.

EPILOGUE

Editing the Arab Spring

Steve Parks, Lindsey Banister, Tamara Issak, Theresa Magdelena Keicher

Revolution By Love, the political movement, began in the living rooms, chat rooms, coffee houses, and classrooms across the Middle East and North Africa. It poured out into the streets of neighborhoods, cities, and capitals. And it produced a transformation in the lives of citizens across the region – a transformation whose impact is still being decided upon and delineated daily.

Revolution By Love, the book, also began in conversation. The discussions among activists, academics, and educators, which took place in person and through social media, concerned the meaning and import of the Arab Spring. These conversations, which captured a particular historical moment in the process, a particular configuration on how the forces for change were emerging and consolidating across the region, also demonstrated how common beliefs and values informed much of their work. It is the recording of these common values embedded in a diversity of experience which this book has so eloquently captured.

And while any book is by its very nature an incomplete representation, we want to use this final chapter as a way of discussing what we have learned by working with these individuals on this project. For while it would be grandiose to claim a book could be as transformative as actions on the ground, the work of completing *Revolution By Love* has left an impact on how we consider our work as U.S. based researchers and teachers – as individuals engaged in the world of education but necessarily understanding our work extends beyond the confines of our classroom.

What follows, then, are some tentative conclusions about the meaning and import of such collaborative efforts.

Publishing Voices

The voices represented in this book are personal, political, and powerful. They are also edited. We worked with each author as they crafted their story, offering insights into how a U.S.-audience need to hear additional facts and more context within a piece. We debated how key terms, such as democracy or struggle, might translate into the dynamics of U.S. classrooms. And throughout, we worked collaboratively to insure that any final version also would be able to speak to the residents of the author's home country. The goal, that is, was to use the editing process of a book to demonstrate how through committed discussion, a common sense of audience, of purpose, might also be crafted. While the book's reception will ultimately determine the success of these efforts, we would argue that the necessity of such committed collaboration should mark any publication project which brings together U.S. academics with academics, activists, and educators across the Middle East and North Africa. Publishing voices should represent, then, a moment in a continual effort to collaborate across histories, borders, and conflicts.

Shifting Identities

It is too easy, however, to bifurcate the partnership in this collaboration, however. While each of us might be characterized by our geographical location – U.S./ Middle East/North Africa – the personal experience of our collective histories endlessly asked us to rethink our own identity. We were more than just "U.S." or "Middle Eastern, "Christian or Muslim." Indeed, at any one moment we might inhabit multiple identities, multiple locations within a conversation or within a moment in a text. Understanding and working within the cross-hatching of histories enabled a richer sense of exploration than if rigid boundaries had been kept in place. Indeed working to insure such a complex vision emerged in this collection demanded care, commitment, and consultation among all of our partners. And we have learned that such writerly identities do not emerge organically, but must be created through the hard work of creating "the sentence," "the paragraph," and then "the chapter." We believe, however, such a collective effort enabled a deeper sense of partnership to emerge and be formed, a partnership based on the production of a printed word but expanding outwards toward friendship and common goals.

Maintaining Alliances

Finally, we believe our work should not end with one publication. For while *Revolution By Love* represents one moment in a conversation, such partnerships should build off such successes. For that reason, this publication will ultimately be part of a larger effort to build upon the possibilities of social media to create a space where the conversation can continue, where possibilities inherent in the book can become reality in the classrooms and communities discussed. For the primary lesson to be learned from the voices in this book is that change does not come quickly nor easily, but must be worked for daily in the small spaces of a classroom, the effort to reform a neighborhood election, and the slow stitching together of such moments into national progress. It is towards this longer effort a systemic change that our collaboration ultimately points.

Our work, then, is not complete. In many ways, it is just beginning. We count ourselves fortunate, however, to have found ourselves engaged with such committed partners, to have discovered and helped nurture a community which supports not only the idea of progress but the individuals active in such work. For within the context of the U.S. academy, "love" might seem a soft word, unconnected to the rigor of theory, to research. Yet as these voices demonstrate, "love" can demand a rigorous commitment in the face of chaos; it can require a theoretical understanding to understand how to proceed in the context of a massive upheaval and violent counterattack. And as the voices in this collection demonstrate, it is only through such an emotional commitment that collective will can sustain itself, insuring positive collective change can occur.

And that is a lesson we hope to draw into our own classrooms, our research, and our professional goals in the years to come.

BIOGRAPHIES

of the writers, as arranged in the book

Book website: www.revolutionbylove.com

Name: Amal Matar
Nationality: Bahraini

Dr. Matar is an ophthalmologist and one of the founder and active members of Bahrain Rehabilitation and Anti-violence Organization (BRAVO) that aims at documentation, rehabilitation and providing legal assistance to torture victims.

She is interested in Islamic feminism and in progressive and modern Islamic interpretations that support the principles of democracy, equality and freedom.

Name: Ibrahim Yousif Shebani
Nationality: Libyan

Mr. Shebani is the Chief Editor and the founder of "The Libyan" magazine, a political, security, economy, culture and arts magazine that started publishing after the February 17th revolution.

Mr. Shebani is interested in learning more about democracy and incorporating this knowledge through the magazine in order to promote democratic principles in Libya.

Name: Dala Ghandour
Nationality: Lebanese
Email: dalaghandour@gmail.com

Ms. Ghandour is a lawyer specialized in family status legal matters and is a certified mediator. Since 2009, she has been developing the mediation culture, as she believes in its power to resolve conflicts & restore relationships. She has been offering her mediation services to the unprivileged populations in North Lebanon with the American Bar Association, as an instructor in Lebanese jails & and as a family mediator for divorced couples, in Beirut Charia Courts. She aims to introduce mediation into the legal system and spread this culture of forgiveness & reconciliation in the Lebanese society. She is the head of the Lebanese mediation Center at the Chamber of Commerce of Beirut and Mount Lebanon.

Interested in empowering youth and women to participate in their own political process and be engaged in the public field, she ran as an independent candidate for Beirut municipality elections in 2010. She believes that politics should not be only left to politicians.

Dala holds a degree in Public & Private Law and a Master in Management, from Lebanon & France.

Name: Samah Elmeri
Nationality: Libyan
Email: samahelmeri@hotmail.com

Ms. Elmeri is a University of Iowa graduate with a bachelor's degree in International studies and Business. Upon liberation of her hometown, Tripoli, she became involved in civil society activities, where she has participated in various conferences, workshops and seminars as well as volunteered with NGO's that have a special concentration on women's issues.

In June 2012, she was in charge of media monitoring of the first Libyan elections working with the European Union Election Assessment Team. Currently she holds the position of Communications and M&E Officer at CREATIVE (Community Driven Grants Program) in Tripoli. One of her contributions this year was writing for Search for Common Ground on how religion is far less divisive in Libya than tribalism.

Ms. Elmeri is interested in the empowerment of Libya's youth especially in the decision making process of democracy building in Libya.

Name: Shatha Al-Harazi
Nationality: Yemeni
Email: shatha.yt@gmail.com
Twitter: @ShathaALHarazi

Ms. Al-Harazi is a Human Rights journalist and political reporter. She worked for the Yemen Times, the first independent English speaking newspaper in Yemen, and is a freelance journalist who has published extensively in the Middle East and Europe. Last June, she was awarded, among nine international women, the Global Trailblazing award by Vital Voices.

Ms. Al-Harazi is also a member of the International Press Institute, which has worked on defending freedom of speech for the last 60 years. Ms. Al-Harazi is also a chairman of a youth initiative called "Inclusion" that works on promoting transparency, monitory and youth political participation; meanwhile she works on a project on monitoring the Yemeni government performance.

Name: Mirelle Karam Halim
Nationality: Egyptian
Email: mirelle_karam@hotmail.com

Ms. Halim is an operations manager for Creative Associates International and has served as a logistics and program officer with the International Foundation for Electoral Systems, whose mission is to increase political awareness and to promote civic engagement. She was chosen to be one of the Young Mediterranean Leaders by European Training Foundation-EU Organization.

Ms. Halim's focus is to work with other local NGOs in Egypt to promote civic engagement and to empower women and youth to participate in the political system.

Name: Raghda Abushahla
Nationality: Palestinian
Email: raghda1979@yahoo.com

Ms. Abushahla is currently working for UNRWA in Gaza, and has previously worked as a translator for the Middle East Office of the United Nations Office for Projects' Services (UNOPS). She has also worked as a British Council liaison to the Palestinian Ministry of Health, working on various projects, such as "Strengthening Health Management" and "Hospital Sector Planning and Management."

Ms. Abushahla is interested in democratization, peaceful political reform and conflict resolution and she hopes to share and apply that knowledge in Gaza.

Name: Emna Ben Yedder
Nationality: Tunisian
Email: ebenyedder@gmail.com

Emna Ben Yedder (Tunisia) is a manager in Mergers & Acquisitions at SWICORP, a corporate finance advisory, private equity and principal investment firm with a specific regional focus on the Middle East and North Africa (MENA).

Since she joined SWICORP in 2007, Emna has been involved in various financial advisory assignments ranging from several acquisitions, greenfield, and joint venture projects to sale mandates. Before joining the group, she gained two years experience as a financial modeling analyst for ABN Amro in London. In her personal time, Emna is also an activist working with an NGO she helped found called "ACT – Think & Decide".

Along with five other NGOs and independents, ACT has implemented a project in Tunisia called Bus Citoyen of which she is the treasurer, which focuses on raising political awareness among citizens and encouraging civil society participation in the democratic transition process and the constitutional writing process. Emna is also a founding member of the "Citizens' Association of Carthage", a residents association created to foster local governance.

She holds a Masters in Business specializing in finance from the Rouen Business School. Emna speaks Arabic, English, French and Spanish.

Name: Salma Nazzal
Nationality: Palestinian
Email: salmanazzal@gmail.com

Ms. Nazzal is currently pursuing a Master's Degree in Democracy and Human Rights at Birzeit University, recently started working with a local NGO in her city of Jenin on a project implemented in partnership with Aman Transparency Palestine. The project works on creating a platform designed to promote the values of integrity, principles of transparency and systems of accountability among institutions in Jenin area.

Prior working with Omniah, Ms. Nazzal worked on Model Schools Network Program. A project administered by AMIDEAST in partnership with the Palestinian Ministry of Education, this project seeks to build institutional capacity in the Palestinian school system. Ms. Nazzal also worked with the Palestinian Red Crescent Society, and served as an interpreter for the Canadian Observation Mission for the Legislative Council Elections, under the umbrella of the UNDP. She is particularly interested in democratic reform, and in helping democracy-promoting NGOs in West Bank expand their geographical reach.

Name: Ahmed Abdelhakim Hachelaf
Nationality: Algerian
Email: ahmedhachelaf@gmail.com

Mr. AbdelHakim has been a volunteer and IT manager for the "Elamel" National Association for Citizen Development, which fights illiteracy and teaches women and the elderly IT skills. He also started an English Club in the Ecole Normale Superior in Algiers, which seeks to promote English language skills and social and leadership skills, as well as democratic values through its horizontal decision-making structure.

Mr. AbdelHakim's goal is to reshape the goals of education in Algeria and to incorporate more civic education and service learning into the curriculum.

Name: Shadin Hamaideh
Nationality: Jordanian
Email: shamaideh@yahoo.com

B.Sc. in Chemical Engineering and MBA.

Ms. Hamaideh is the Director of the Inspirational and Career Guidance Program at INJAZ in Jordan, a member nation of Junior Achievement Worldwide®.

Prior to INJAZ (2004 – 2006), Ms. Hamaideh was a Part-time Teacher and a Story Board Writer at several schools and firms that work on creating, developing and digitalizing e-learning curricula and provide solutions and multimedia content.

Prior to the above (2001-2004), Ms. Hamaideh worked in the shipping and logistics industry, with one of the world's biggest companies, where she coordinated some shipping solutions, online and e-commerce services in Jordan and around the world.

Ms. Hamaideh is a member in the Career Guidance Committee of the E-TVET Council Secretariat, in addition to being a Certified Trainer and Consultant for Jordan Career Education Foundation-JCEF and Education for Employment Foundation-EFE.

Name: Mohammed Masbah
Nationality: Moroccan
Email: masbahmohammed@yahoo.fr

Mr. Masbah is a Ph.D. Fellow in the project "Elite change and new social mobilization in the Arab world" at Stiftung Wissenschaft und Politik (SWP) - Berlin, he is also a Ph. D. candidate in sociology at Mohammad V. University in Rabat and a researcher at the Moroccan Center for Contemporary Studies and Research, where he also served as the editor of the 2nd report on the Religious Situation in Morocco and the co-director of a project on youth and religiosity in Morocco. He served as an expert for the Moroccan Minister of Communication, and was recently a visiting researcher at the Carnegie Endowment for International Peace in Washington D.C.

Name: Muna Abbas Ali AlBuloushi
Nationality: Kuwaiti
Email: muna.albuloushi@hotmail.com

Ms. AlBuloushi is a middle school teacher who has taught both English and Arabic for various international programs. She is interested in politics and democratization in order to become involved in the political process in Kuwait.

In particular, she wants to help improve the relations between the government of Kuwait and the National Assembly and promote more inclusive political institutions. As well as helping young citizen to understand their civic rights and be well educated civically. She believes development of a country comes from the development of the individuals.

Ms. Albuloushi seeks every available chance to develop her own political views in order to develop her country. Her personal view of a successful country is to run it fairly by applying firm rules, freedom of speech and respectful well educated National Assembly members.

ACKNOWLEDGEMENTS

We would like to thank and express our deepest gratitude to Dr. Julia Ganson, Executive Education at the Maxwell School, who believed in us and our project when it was still just a vague idea. Forever Grateful!

We would also like to thank and extend our warmest regards to Dr. Steve Parks, Lindsey Banister, Tamara Issak, and Theresa Magdelena Keicher at the Composition and Cultural Rhetoric Program, College of Arts and Sciences for support and help in the editing process; but, more so, we would like to thank Dr. Parks for encouraging us to believe more in the power of our voices, for boosting our energies and morale, and invigorating our passion during this project. This book would not have been possible without him.

Thanks given to everybody that supported us to be what we are.

Last but not least, we would like to thank each one who participated in this wonderful adventure: We feel blessed that fate put us all together.